ESSENTIALS OF WESLEYAN THEOLOGY

A Contemporary Affirmation

Paul A. Mickey

ZONDERVAN
PUBLISHING HOUSE OF THE ZONDERVAN CORPORATION
GRAND RAPIDS, MICHIGAN 49506

31925

ESSENTIALS OF WESLEYAN THEOLOGY

Copyright © 1980 by The Zondervan Corporation
Grand Rapids, Michigan

Library of Congress Cataloging in Publication Data

Mickey, Paul A 1937–
     Essentials of Wesleyan theology.

     (Contemporary evangelical persepectives)
     Includes text of the Junaluska Affirmation of Scriptural Christianity for United
Methodists.
     Includes bibliographical references and index.   1. Junaluska Affirmation of
Scriptural Christianity for United Methodists. 2. Methodist Church—Doctrinal and
controversial works—Methodist authors. 3. United Methodist Church (United
States) 4. Evangelicalism—United States. I. Woodworth, Ralph. II. Terpstra,
Gerard. III. Junaluska Affirmation of Scriptural Christianity for United Methodists.
IV. Title.

BX8331.2.M48   230'.76   80-17410
ISBN 0-310-39151-2

Unless otherwise indicated, Scripture quotations are from the Holy Bible, New
International Version, copyright © 1978 by New York International Bible Society.
Used by permission.

Edited by Ralph Woodworth and Gerard Terpstra
Designed by Paul M. Hillman and Stanley N. Gundry

Printed in the United States of America

ESSENTIALS OF WESLEYAN THEOLOGY

To my parents,
Ellen S. Mickey
and
Martin E. Mickey,
who nurtured me on
the essentials of
Evangelical,
Evangelical United Brethren,
and United Methodist
theology

Contents

Foreword

At the turn of the fourth century Christianity was still underground, a persecuted remnant. The greatest problem for the church, however, was not that she was a remnant, nor was it even the persecution she endured. The greatest problem was that the remnant was divided. Christians in hiding have very little contact with one another. Then, with the conversion of Constantine and the signing of the Edict of Milan, Christians were suddenly free to express their faith openly. Many beliefs surfaced almost at once. The church was forced to come together to affirm a common faith. Thus, the councils and their resulting creeds were formed to articulate the faith for those times. The goal: a remnant united under the banner of "scriptural Christianity."

Again Christians find themselves at such a point in history. It is the "in thing" to be a Christian. Renewal groups are flourishing. Within United Methodism, however, much of the theology that has surfaced in an age of pluralism is just as diverse as that of the fourth century. The "Junaluska Affirmation"—"a statement of essential beliefs in a Wesleyan-oriented theology"—attempts to reestablish biblical, historical roots. The goal: a remnant united under the banner of "scriptural Christianity."

Dr. Mickey provides a solid, workable commentary for the recently drafted "Junaluska Affirmation" in the form of a positive evangelical witness. The words *scriptural Christianity* introducing that document do not imply that it is divinely inspired, as if to add to the biblical corpus. They do imply, however, that it is an honest, straightforward attempt to represent the Scriptures fairly within the Wesleyan tradition. I trust Paul Mickey. I find here no hidden agenda, no grinding of the proverbial axe, and no polemic.

Furthermore, this book not only touches the biblical base but also struggles with the history of our movement. John

Wesley's theology, however, was formulated at the crossroads of scholarship and ministry, education and experience, theory and practice. For that reason few have attempted the monumental task of presenting Wesleyan/Arminian theology in the form of a systematic that communicates the essence of evangelical truth from a sound biblical base. This commentary on the "Junaluska Affirmation" provides Dr. Mickey with the opportunity to accept that challenge.

United Methodists have been accused of being long on experience and short on theology. The fact is that United Methodism is a pluralistic, nonconfessional church. There is no creed that one must adhere to in order to become a United Methodist. There are no unique doctrines or experiences normative for United Methodists other than those essential to the biblical understanding of salvation. Pluralism should ensure freedom and adaptability. We cannot, however, afford to become so broadminded that we become flatheaded. Wesley himself insisted that with regard to certain doctrines "we think and let think"—*but only outside essentials.* Dr. Mickey, therefore, presents a frank discussion of doctrines essential for scriptural Christianity. Potentially controversial doctrines—involving, for example, the inspiration of Scripture, the historicity of Jesus (His birth, death, resurrection, glorification, and return), the atonement, and perfection (a watchword among early Methodists)—are taken head-on with a clarity and vitality that is entirely refreshing.

Dr. Mickey also exhibits balance. For example, John Calvin is quoted extensively, not by way of contrast so much as to demonstrate an appreciation of the historical precedents for our evangelical heritage. The author never succumbs to the arid orthodoxy common to the neo-Calvinistic scholasticism of some dogmatic theologians.

The tone of the book is not argumentative. The commentary is not pitted against any particular persuasion. Dr. Mickey does, however, encourage the kind of tough reflection that refuses to theologize by default. Not to decide is to decide. Using terms that can be understood by the contemporary mind, he provides United Methodists with a clear understanding of their biblical faith.

So this book not only provides a systematic approach to theology from the Wesleyan/Arminian perspective but it does so in such a way that it is profitable reading for clergy and laity alike. It is an excellent reference work as well. The outline is so transparent that any student can turn to the sections that are applicable to a particular interest and read profitably. Questions at the end of each chapter make this a useful tool for study groups, lay academies, and church school classes. In addition, the work is not so heavily documented as to inhibit its flow and continuity. Its documentation, however, is more than adequate to provide the serious student with leads for further study.

This is a welcomed book. It will be a valued addition to any library. Buy it, read it, mark it, use it, recommend it.

Robert G. Tuttle, Jr.
Tulsa, Oklahoma

Preface

The life, theology, zeal, and intellectual influence of John Wesley, Anglican reformer of the eighteenth century and founder of what has become known as Methodism, are of abiding significance for Christendom. The corpus of Wesley's contribution cannot be contained by his *Journal* or the Thirty-nine Articles of Religion or his *Explanatory Notes on the New Testament* or his *Sermons* or hymns or leadership in the establishing of Methodism in the United States. Wesleyan theology occupies, strangely enough, a rather precarious position in the current theological atmosphere of United Methodism. Increasingly one discovers appeals to the ambiguity of "our Methodist heritage" but fewer and fewer direct appeals to the theological clarity and intentionality of Wesley's ministry and writings. Nearly a century has passed since a theology based on the essentials of Wesley's thought has been pursued. It is regretful but necessary to observe that a precipitating factor in the preparation of this volume emanates from theological conflict.

This study originated as a theological statement growing out of a Wesleyan-oriented evangelical renewal movement, the Good News Movement, "A Forum for Scriptural Christianity within the United Methodist Church." It is a spontaneous grass-roots evangelical renaissance within American Methodism. Good News people were continually being asked, "Well, what do those who claim to be evangelicals and claim to be deeply influenced by Wesley's theology actually say for themselves now, in the late twentieth century?"

A task force was commissioned to present to the full Board of Directors of Good News a statement of the essential beliefs in a Wesleyan-oriented theology. The statement known as the Junaluska Affirmation was adopted at Lake Junaluska, North Carolina, a summer activities center of the United Methodist Church.

9

The spirit of the statement is to witness to the primacy of Scripture among the theological authorities for the Christian. The Scriptures are the foundation for Christian doctrine and practice in daily life. Each section of the statement therefore is introduced by the phrase *Scriptural Christianity affirms.* The tone of the statement is intended to be positive in its evangelical witness.

The Affirmation is a demonstration that evangelicals can unite in gracious but firm spirit to declare essential, core beliefs. The witness of the Junaluska Affirmation is offered openly to any who desire to examine the living discipline of scriptural Christianity. In the hope of evoking an affirming witness to the essentials of Wesleyan theology, this commentary has been prepared.

The format of this study follows that of the Affirmation, with chapters on each of the sections, including the Preamble. This commentary does not pretend to exhaust the truth, intention, or reality of scriptural Christianity. Its primary purpose is to affirm and commend the scriptural Christianity formulated and taught by John Wesley.

Acknowledgments

I wish to express my deep debt to my colleagues on the task force who helped to prepare the Junaluska Affirmation: Riley B. Case, James V. Heidinger, Charles W. Keysor, Dennis F. Kinlaw, Lawrence H. Souder, Frank Bateman Stanger, and Robert J. Stamps. To my wife, Jane, goes my fondest admiration for weathering the time and travel needed to prepare the Affirmation and to write this commentary. A discerning lay theologian in her own right, Jane has made a gracious contribution to this effort to affirm scriptural Christianity. My spirit and mind have been boosted throughout the long period of manuscript preparation by those who have read it and, with patience and grace, offered their constructive criticisms: John B. Cobb, Jr., Charles W. Keysor, Albert C. Outler, Robert C. Price, and Mark R. Branson. Helpful assistance came from the adult education class of Bel Air Presbyterian Church, Los Angeles, during our Sunday morning study of this commentary. My appreciation is extended also to my secretary, Jacquelyn P. Norris, who has labored faithfully over the years required to complete this project.

THE JUNALUSKA AFFIRMATION

of Scriptural Christianity for United Methodists

PREAMBLE

In a time of theological pluralism, Good News and other evangelicals within United Methodism have thought it necessary to reaffirm the historic faith of the Church. Our theological understanding of this faith has been expressed in the Apostles' Creed, Nicene Creed, and in John Wesley's standard *Sermons* and the *Explanatory Notes upon the New Testament.* We affirm in their entirety the validity and integrity of these expressions of Scriptural truth, and recognize them as the doctrinal standards of our denomination.

We also recognize that our situation calls for a contemporary restatement of these truths. The merging of two great traditions, the Evangelical United Brethren and the Methodist, with their two authentic witnesses to the historic faith, *The Confession of Faith* and *The Articles of Religion*, gives further occasion for such a statement. Moreover, we recognize the mandate which the doctrinal statement of the 1972 General Conference has placed upon "all its members to accept the challenge of responsible theological reflection."

Consequently, we offer to the United Methodist Church this theological affirmation of Scriptural Christianity.

THE HOLY TRINITY

Scriptural Christianity affirms the existence of the one Eternal God who has revealed Himself as Father, Son and Holy Spirit, three equal but distinct Persons, mysteriously united in the Godhead which the Church historically has described as the Holy Trinity.

GOD THE FATHER

Scriptural Christianity affirms that the first Person of the Holy Trinity, God the Father, is the Eternal One and reigns supremely. He has provided a covenant through which His

14

creatures can be redeemed and through which His creation will be liberated from all evil and brought to final righteousness at the end of the age.

GOD THE SON

Scriptural Christianity affirms that the second Person of the Holy Trinity, the Eternal Son, became incarnate as Mary's virgin-born Child, Jesus of Nazareth, the Christ. In His unique Person, He revealed to us both the fullness of deity and the fullness of humanity. By His life, suffering, death, resurrection and ascension He provided the only way of salvation. His sacrifice on the cross once and for all was to reconcile the Holy God and sinners, thus providing the only way of access to the Father. Now He intercedes as High Priest before the Father, awaiting the day when He will return to judge every person, living and dead, and to consummate His Kingdom.

GOD THE HOLY SPIRIT

Scriptural Christianity affirms that the third Person of the Holy Trinity, the Holy Spirit, was active from the beginning

15

in creation, revelation and redemption. It was through His anointing that prophets received the Word of God, priests became intermediaries between God and His people, and kings were given ruling authority. The Spirit's presence and power, measured in the Old Testament, were found without measure in Jesus of Nazareth, the Anointed. The Spirit convicts and woos the lost, gives new birth to the penitent, and abides in the believer, perfecting holiness and empowering the Church to carry out Christ's mission in the world. He came to indwell His Church at Pentecost, enabling believers to yield fruit and endowing them with spiritual gifts according to His will. He bears witness to Christ and guides God's people into His truth. He inspired the Holy Scriptures, God's written Word, and continues to illuminate His people concerning His will and truth. His guidance is always in harmony with Christ and the truth as given in the Holy Scriptures.

HUMANITY

Scriptural Christianity affirms that man and woman are fashioned in the image of God and are different from all of God's other creatures. God intends that we should glorify Him and enjoy Him forever. Since the Fall of Adam the corruption of sin has pervaded every person and extended into social relationships, societal systems, and all creation. This corruption is so pervasive that we are not capable of positive response to God's offer of redemption, except by the prevenient, or preparing, grace of God. Only through the justifying, regenerating and sanctifying work of the Triune God can we be saved from the corruption of sin, become increasingly conformed to the image of Christ, and be restored to the relationships which God has intended for us.

THE HOLY SCRIPTURES

Scriptural Christianity affirms as the only written Word of God the Old and New Testaments. These Holy Scriptures contain all that is necessary for our knowledge of God's holy and sovereign will, of Jesus Christ the only Redeemer, of our salvation, and of our growth in grace. They are to be received through the Holy Spirit as the guide and final authority for the faith and conduct of individuals and the doctrines and life of the Church. Whatever is not clearly revealed in, or plainly established as truth by, the Holy Scriptures cannot be required as an article of faith nor be taught as essential to salvation. Anything contrary to the teachings of the Holy Scriptures is contrary to the purposes of God and must, therefore, be opposed. The authority of Scripture derives from the fact that God, through His Spirit, inspired the authors, causing them to perceive God's truth and record it with accuracy. It is evident that the Holy Scriptures have been preserved during the long process of transmission through copyists and translators, and we attribute such accurate preservation to the work of the Holy Spirit. These Scriptures are supremely authoritative for the Church's teaching, preaching, witness, identifying error, correcting the erring, and training believers for ministry in and through the Church.

SALVATION

Scriptural Christianity affirms that God offers salvation to a sinful humanity and a lost world through Jesus Christ. By His death on the cross the sinless Son propitiated the holy wrath of the Father, a righteous anger occasioned by sin. By His resurrection from the dead, the glorified Son raises us to newness of life. When we appropriate by faith God's atoning work in Jesus Christ we are forgiven, justified, regenerated by His Holy Spirit, and adopted into the family of God. By His grace He sanctifies His children, purifying their hearts by faith, renewing them in the image of God, and enabling them to love God and neighbor with whole heart. The fullness of God's great salvation will come with the return of Christ. This cosmic event will signal the resurrection of the saved to eternal life and the lost to eternal damnation, the liberation of creation from the Adamic curse, God's final victory over every power and dominion, and the establishment of the new heaven and the new earth.

THE CHURCH

Scriptural Christianity affirms that the Church of Jesus Christ is the community of all true believers under His

18

sovereign Lordship. This Church, the Body of Christ, is *one* because it shares one Lord, one faith, one baptism. It is *holy* because it belongs to God and is set apart for His purposes in the world. It is *apostolic* because it partakes of the authority granted to the apostles by Christ Himself. It is *universal* because it includes all believers, both living and dead, in every nation, regardless of denominational affiliation. Its authenticity is to be found wherever the pure Word of God is preached and taught; wherever the Sacraments of Baptism and Holy Communion are celebrated in obedience to Christ's command; wherever the gifts of the Holy Spirit upbuild the body and bring spiritual growth; wherever the Spirit of God creates a loving, caring fellowship, and a faithfulness in witness and service to the world; and wherever discipline is administered with love under the guidance of the Word of God. The Church, as the Bride of Christ, will ultimately be joined with her Lord in triumphant glory.

ETHICS

Scriptural Christianity affirms that we are God's workmanship, created in Christ Jesus for good works. These works are the loving expressions of gratitude by the believer for the new life received in Christ. They do not earn one's salvation nor are they a substitute for God's work of redemption. Rather, they are the result of regeneration and are manifest in the believer as evidence of a living faith.

God has called us to do justice, to love kindness, and to walk humbly with Him. In the Scriptures are found the standards and principles that guide the believer in this walk.

These ethical imperatives, willingly accepted by the believer, enable us to be a part of God's purposes in the world. Moreover, in this we are called to an obedience that does not stop short of our willingness to suffer for righteousness' sake, even unto death.

Our life in Christ includes an unstinting devotion to deeds of kindness and mercy and a wholehearted participation in collective efforts to alleviate need and suffering. The believer will work for honesty, justice and equity in human affairs; all of which witness to inherent rights and a basic dignity common to all persons created in the image of God. Such contemporary issues as racism, housing, welfare, education, Marxism, capitalism, hunger, crime, sexism, family relationships, aging, sexuality, drugs and alcohol, abortion, leisure, pornography, and related issues call for prayerful consideration, thoughtful analysis, and appropriate action from Christians, and must always be a matter of concern to the Church. Thus, we remember that faith without works is dead.

July 20, 1975   Lake Junaluska, North Carolina

PREAMBLE

In a time of theological pluralism, Good News and other evangelicals within United Methodism have thought it necessary to reaffirm the historic faith of the Church. Our theological understanding of this faith has been expressed in the Apostles' Creed, Nicene Creed, and in John Wesley's standard Sermons *and the* Explanatory Notes upon the New Testament. *We affirm in their entirety the validity and integrity of these expressions of Scriptural truth, and recognize them as the doctrinal standards of our denomination.*

We also recognize that our situation calls for a contemporary restatement of these truths. The merging of two great traditions, the Evangelical United Brethren and the Methodist, with their two authentic witnesses to the historic faith, The Confession of Faith *and* The Articles of Religion, *gives further occasion for such a statement. Moreover, we recognize the mandate which the doctrinal statement of the 1972 General Conference has placed upon "all its members to accept the challenge of responsible theological reflection."*

Consequently, we offer to the United Methodist Church this theological affirmation of Scriptural Christianity.

THEOLOGICAL AFFIRMATIONS AND PLURALISM

All significant events emerge from a historical context that anticipates their coming and helps carry their flow into the future. A preamble is an effort to be specific about the particulars of that context. The evangelical awakening and the emergence of organized evangelical renewal groups within the mainline Protestant denominations in the United States, such as the United Methodist, the United Presbyterian USA, the United Presbyterian U.S., and the Episcopal Church, reflect a deep theological struggle. The current crisis is one of so-called theological pluralism. The term *theological pluralism* outdistances any traditional disagreements among the liberals and conservatives. It is distinguished by what it does not affirm, quite unlike the well-defined battle lines drawn in the fights between liberal and orthodox theology of previous generations. Traditionally, theological controversy arises when claims for resolving specific theological conflicts cannot be reconciled in a manner that allows both parties to retain their integrity in the midst of the reconciliation. Those holding to theological pluralism, however, most vehemently claim that each boundary, or limit, is superseded by yet another possibility.[1] Hence, ultimately, no boundary can long endure. In fact, endurance itself is suspect. Therefore, nothing that endures can be affirmed or claimed.

None of the major American Protestant groups have gone so far as to claim theological pluralism, in the functional sense described above, as an official confessional position. But functionally and operationally theological pluralism is in virulent evidence among the denominations; it encourages theological assent to, and support of, the slogan "Anything goes except enduring essentials."

Confusion over the limits of theological pluralism is the background and historical setting out of which the various contemporary evangelical renewal groups have come to life. Theological pluralism tends to create a persuasion that is evidenced by what one is not against rather than what one affirms as essential to Christian faith. Some would have us adopt a type of pluralism orthodoxy: if one affirms anything short of a pluralism or "anything goes" principle, one is open to the charge of exclusivism. Such a person lacks a truly inclusive spirit. Thus, some critics of the evangelical renewal groups perceive them as divisive, haughty, and exclusivistic. Insofar as the spirit of pluralistic orthodoxy endeavors to include everything that sounds theological, it can affirm little that has abiding integrity.

Dead confessional orthodoxy is the seedbed out of which both pluralism and evangelical renewal arise. Evangelicals are concerned to affirm the historic faith of the church. The intent of this activity is to affirm a faith that is alive and well in the present day. The goal is not to hide behind orthodoxy. Pluralism too is an effort to move beyond dead orthodoxy, to be open and inclusive.

The renewal groups are composed chiefly of lay people and parish ministers. In short, these are grass-roots movements. Their primary concern in affirming the historic faith of the church is to feed the spiritually hungry and biblically starved people in the church constituency. The evangelical renewal groups can hardly be dismissed as a rear-guard action of a reactionary political and economic conservatism.[2] Many in the church see theological pluralism as indiscriminate inclusiveness in trivia, incidentals, and innovations. It is chaff. It cannot thrive on the gospel of Jesus Christ alone. The evangelical renewal groups in the various denominations have emerged precisely because their constituencies want to have their life and ministry based on a lively faith and firm theological foundation.

Some would disband the renewal groups as divisive and separatist because they seek theological clarity and spiritual feeding. The renewalists, however, claim that from the beginning theirs is a constructive theological work within mainline denominations.

THE BASIS FOR AFFIRMATION

The evangelical church renewal movement has as its starting point the historic faith of the church. The call for renewal beckons the various denominations to a return to the Scriptures, the creeds, and the great truths of the Reformation as essential core for doctrine. Alongside the summons to these theological expressions of faith is the invitation to affirm the personal appropriation of grace—conversion and the new life—that flows from and adds to the new birth. This new life is an experience of the whole person and is evidenced in a clear demonstration of an active social conscience rooted in the Scriptures.

The call to Wesleyan essentials is a call to a clearly understood doctrinal position without being doctrinaire and to a lively social witness without being faddish. The first step is to affirm a theological center in the midst of theological confusion or outright antagonism toward the historic faith of the church. One begins this task by affirming the faith of the church universal. This faith is clearly evidenced in the classic creeds and the works of the Reformers—John Calvin, Martin Luther, John Knox, John Wesley, Philip Otterbein, Jacob Albright, and others. In this study Wesley's works constitute the primary doctrinal linkage with the mainstream of Christendom; but they cannot be accepted as a substitute that would discard other theological reflections and creeds of the church. Theological affirmations such as the Apostles' Creed, the Nicene Creed, and the work of Reformers such as Calvin and Luther are specific instances of what is being claimed by an appeal to the historic faith of the church.

What Wesley claimed as scriptural Christianity has enjoyed a dominant and extended sweep from biblical times to the present. The doctrinal building blocks of this historic faith help to secure and extend the faith and witness of evangelicals. The writings of the historic faith are expressions of scriptural truth and are therefore acknowledged as authoritative for the evangelical and the various denominations in which evangelical renewal is being effected.

The creeds, affirmations, studies, and reflections on the Holy Scriptures are based on a partial witness to scriptural truth. They are, nevertheless, adequate and faithful to the eternal truths revealed in the Scriptures and in Jesus Christ. Tradition is always subordinate to, and finally dependent on, the authority of Scripture and scriptural truth.

Doctrinal standards, like John the Baptist, always point to the truth of God's revelation in His Son, Jesus Christ. Doctrine is an expression of the truth revealed in Jesus Christ and the Holy Scriptures and is essential to the faith walk in Jesus Christ.

Believers affirm the validity and integrity of these traditions of the historic faith and bear faithful witness to their spiritual ancestors, the saints of the church. The gospel tradition is passed along through the life of the church. Evangelicals are not to take from whatever theological source they may happen to find appealing, regardless of surface attractiveness.

Expressions of scriptural truth and doctrinal standards are available to the church universal and the evangelical because there is a common witness. The doctrinal fountainhead out of which the classic and historic expressions of the faith flow is precisely the community of the faithful, the witness of the redeemed, and the reflection of the pilgrims to that promised land. Into that stream of faithful witnesses the Junaluska Affirmation is offered to accompany the communion of saints and the cloud of witnesses who have prepared the way.

WHAT DO EVANGELICALS BELIEVE?

Frequently the new convert wants a new theology as well as a new life in Christ. Being born again includes the whole person, the mind and intellect along with the spirit and emotions. The question "What do evangelicals believe?" is pressed by new believers and by those who seek to understand the "new evangelicalism."

Following the merger of the former Methodist and Evangelical United Brethren (EUB) churches in 1968, many were asking of that new denomination, "What do you believe?" That is a good question. What are the essentials of Wesleyan theology that guide people today? To answer that question, the Junaluska Affirmation was prepared and offered initially to the United Methodist constituency and to all who were interested in evangelical renewal. To date the Junaluska Affirmation stands as a unique testimony within the American evangelical community. Obviously a number of contemporary theologians are publishing widely from the evangelical perspective.[3] But none of these writings has been produced by persons or groups deeply involved in the daily struggles of the various evangelical renewal movements within the mainline denominations. The Junaluska Affirmation and this commentary were called forth out of the need for a contemporary restatement of what evangelicals believe and out of the daily struggles of a grass-roots, lay people–oriented, evangelical renewal group.

The author, along with many others involved in the evangelical renewal movements, has engaged in voluminous correspondence, numerous telephone calls, and many local congregational and renewal group meetings where the evangelical theological affirmations fall prey to relentless institutional pressure, misunderstanding, and open discouragement. Some who call themselves evangelical have failed to exhibit a gracious, warm spirit in asserting their beliefs and experience. Sometimes the failure of grace and charity is a result of ignorance, poor education, and a lack of intellectual sophistication. As often as not, the conflict is evoked or provoked by pastors, denominational representatives, and agency committees or actions that take deliberate occasion to oppress openly and/or drive out of the congregational and denominational life those who declare an evangelical theological position.

This study is offered by one openly and actively involved in the corporate as well as the academic dimensions of the evangelical renewal movement within the mainline denominations. It is written with the hope that it will help clarify and educate in all quarters, that it will yield understanding for all, that it will facilitate a heightened mutual respect, and above all that the Lordship of Jesus Christ will be exalted.

DISCUSSION QUESTIONS

1. What are some of the most compelling reasons for a contemporary affirmation of scriptural Christianity?

2. Is such a statement needed any more among United Methodists than among other denominational groups? Why or why not?

3. Some lay people feel they are not trained to prepare theological statements or do not have the right words to write theology. However, what people do as a result of their beliefs is one form of a theological statement. What are some practical ways in which each of us can learn to write our own affirmation of faith?

4. The Junaluska Affirmation challenges us to consider the importance of scriptural Christianity. Is this really important? Why or why not?

5. Is the Junaluska Affirmation a positive sign that evangelical theology is receiving a hearing?

6. Is theological reflection a mandate for the Christian? Is it for you personally?

THE
HOLY TRINITY

Scriptural Christianity affirms the existence of the one Eternal God who has revealed Himself as Father, Son and Holy Spirit, three equal but distinct Persons, mysteriously united in the Godhead which the Church historically has described as the Holy Trinity.

One could expend considerable energy in endless speculations about the existence of God, proving ultimately nothing. There are the classic arguments for the existence of God and other more or less philosophically oriented debates about God's existence. But these tend to lead the believer into purely philosophical speculations and a fascination for philosophical conceptualities.

Scriptural Christianity affirms the existence of the one Eternal God . . .

The evangelical need not indulge in speculation about the existence of God or to affirm God by argument. The evangelical makes initial appeal to the testimony of Holy Scripture, not to philosophical argumentation and the sciences of linguistics and logic. The Scriptures testify to the one true and living God (e.g., 1 Kings 8:60; Isa. 43:10–11; Mark 12:29, 32; 1 Thess. 1:9). God's Word stakes out the starting point for theology and establishes initially the oneness and eternality of God.

God is not a philosophical idea. God is the power over all other powers. God is not a static being or substance dangling at the end of a human conceptual fishing pole. God is the sovereign of and in history.

John Wesley declared in his sermon "On the Trinity" that the Bible bears testimony to the Trinity.[1] Belief is not a speculative philosophical argument. In the sermon Wesley claimed,

> There are many things "which eye hath not seen, nor ear heard, neither hath it entered into the heart of man to conceive." Part of these God hath "revealed to us by his Spirit. . . ."
>
> Now, where is the wisdom of rejecting what is revealed, because we do not understand what is not revealed? of denying the *fact* which God has unveiled, because we cannot see the *manner*, which is veiled still?
>
> Especially when we consider that what God has been pleased to reveal upon this head, is far from being a point of indifference,

is a truth of the last importance. It enters into the very heart of Christianity: It lies at the root of all vital religion.

Unless these Three are One, how can "all men honour the Son, even as they honour the Father"?

"I know not what to do," says Socinus in a letter to his friend, "with my untoward followers: They will not worship Jesus Christ. I tell them it is written 'Let all the angels of God worship him.' They answer, However that be, if he is not God, we dare not worship him. For 'it is written, Thou shalt worship the Lord thy God, and him only shalt thou serve.'"

But the thing which I here particularly mean is this: The knowledge of the Three-One God is interwoven with all true Christian faith; with all vital religion.[2]

One readily notes from this sermon excerpt that argumentation fails to establish the fact of the Trinity. Rather, belief in the Holy Trinity heads the list of affirmations. It is, as Wesley noted, "a truth of the last importance. It enters into the very heart of Christianity: It lies at the root of all vital religion."

Argument can neither establish nor destroy this affirmation. One believes or one does not. Wesley correctly perceived that failure to believe is "far from being a point of indifference." What one believes or fails to believe about the Trinity establishes a specific theological orientation. This orientation—affirming or skeptical—will affect beliefs about the person and work of Christ, the nature of the church, and Christian discipleship.

The formal doctrine of the Holy Trinity emerged from concerns of the early church to live by doctrinal standards that would accurately reflect the testimony of the Scriptures. Scholars remind us that the *kerygma* (teaching, or doctrine) of the New Testament church did not contain a formal doctrine of the Trinity. Although belief in the Triune God may not have been carefully articulated until the Council of Nicea, the reality of the Trinity was assumed as implicitly taught in the Scriptures and it won testimony in the creeds of the church.

Evangelicals join Wesley in a simple affirmation of the one

eternal God, the Triune God. The Trinity is accepted as a matter of record. One affirms what God has revealed without a compulsion to comprehend details God has not revealed.

THE REVEALED TRUTH

That God has revealed Himself as a tri-unity is woven into the very fabric of the Scriptures. John Wesley employed the terms *Trinity* and *persons* to refer to God, and with no hesitation. He cautioned his follow-

... who has revealed Himself ... ers, however, not to insist that others mimic those exact words. In his sermon "On the Trinity," Wesley registered a caution that reflected the serious intensity of the doctrinal debate:

> Much less would I burn a man alive, and that with moist, green wood, for saying, "Though I believe the Father is God, the Son is God, and the Holy Ghost is God; yet I scruple using the words *Trinity* and *Persons*, because I do not find those terms in the Bible."[3]

Wesley used as his text 1 John 5:7 (KJV): "There are three that bear record in heaven, the Father, the Word, and the Holy Ghost: and these three are one." Wesley claimed this as the only overt scriptural teaching on the Trinity. Even though this text is almost certainly not genuine, having appeared only in late manuscripts of the Latin Vulgate, its teaching can be found clearly, though not so succinctly, in other parts of Scripture (e.g., Isa. 61:1 with Luke 4:17–21; Matt. 3:16–17).

The truth revealed about the Trinity is that God enjoys a variety of relationships with the world, using different means to relate Himself to us. The Judeo-Christian faith believes in one God. It is a monotheistic faith. By contrast, polytheism affirms many gods. The Christian believes in the one true and living God, three persons in one Godhead, united mysteriously as Father, Son, and Holy Spirit, coequal and coeternal.

In Wesley's sermon "Catholic Spirit," he raised a basic issue of theological certainty and ministerial trust: "Is thine heart right, as my heart is with thy heart?"[4] Having raised the rhetorical question, Wesley hastened to elaborate:

> The first thing implied is this: Is thy heart right with God? Dost thou believe his being, and his perfections? his eternity, immensity, wisdom, power; his justice, mercy, and truth? Dost thou believe that he now "upholdeth all things by the word of his power?" and that he governs even the most minute, even the most noxious, to his own glory, and the good of them that love him? Hast thou a divine evidence, a supernatural conviction, of the things of God? Dost thou "walk by faith, not by sight?" looking not at temporal things, but things eternal?[5]

Clearly, the question of ministerial trust is predicated on a positive theological affirmation of doctrinal essentials regarding God's being. Central to the affirmation are the experiential attributes—eternity, immensity, wisdom, power, justice, mercy, and truth. "Walking by faith" is just that: it is an experience and not a matter of ideas alone. But the faithful walk is impossible without an anchoring in doctrine. Therefore a second minimal requirement is established for walking hand in hand as believers: belief in the eternal God. Evidence for the attributes mentioned above is seen in the lives of believers and includes a supernatural conviction based on revelation and the testimony of Scripture: we are to "walk by faith, not by sight."

The Christian affirms one God, who reveals Himself, giving guidance in the walk that is by faith and not by sight.

THE UNITY OF THE GODHEAD

The one eternal God is revealed as Father, Son, and Holy Spirit. The unity of the Godhead has been central to the doctrinal understanding of the universal church historically. The Scriptures do not teach explicitly the doctrine of the Holy Trinity, but this affirmation is present throughout. In fact, the theologians of the church, the so-called church fathers, based their theology on the doctrine.

. . . as Father, Son and Holy Spirit . . .

33

In *The Institutes of the Christian Religion* John Calvin claimed this for the Trinity:

> The Scriptural teaching concerning God's infinite and spiritual essence ought to be enough, not only to banish popular delusions, but also to refute the subtleties of secular philosophy. One of the ancients seems aptly to have remarked, "Whatever we see, and whatever we do not see, is God."* According to this, he fancied that divinity was poured out into the various parts of the world. But even if God, to keep us sober, speaks sparingly of his essence, yet by those two titles that I have used [Trinity and Person] he both banishes stupid imaginings and restrains the boldness of the human mind. Surely, his infinity ought to make us afraid to try to measure him by our own senses.[6]

Later in the discussion Calvin stated,

> For He so proclaims himself the sole God as to offer himself to be contemplated clearly in three Persons. Unless we grasp these, only the bare and empty name of God flits about in our brains, to the exclusion of the true God. Again, lest anyone imagine that God is threefold or think that God's simple essence is to be torn into three Persons,† we must here seek a short and easy definition to free us from all error.[7]

---

*(Footnote of J. T. McNeill, editor of *Institutes*:) Seneca, *Natural Questions*, Prologue, I. 13 (tr. J. Clarke, *Physical Science in the Time of Nero*, p. 7).

†(Footnote of J. T. McNeill, editor of *Institutes*:) Calvin here and in sec. 3 alludes to numerous opinions in the works of anti-trinitarian writers of his time. Barth and Niesel have supplied detailed references to writings of Michael Servetus (d. 1553), Mattaeus Gribaldi (d. 1564), George Blandrata (d. 1585), Valentine Gentile (d. 1566), Gianpaulo Alciati (d. 1573). (OS III. 109ff.) For the ideas and activities of these men, see E. M. Wilbur, *A History of Unitarianism: Socinianism and Its Antecedents.* The charge that traditional orthodoxy affirmed a "three-fold God," or "three gods" appears in Servetus, *De Trinitatis Erroribus,* 1531, I, fo. 21 (tr. E. M. Wilbur, *On the Errors of the Trinity* I. 30, 31, pp. 33f.; *Harvard Theological Studies* 16). The later literature of research in this field has been examined by G. H. Williams in LCC (Library of Christian Classics) XXV. 285ff. and in "Studies in the Radical Reformation: A Bibliographical Survey of Research Since 1939," *Church History* XXVII (1958), 46–49.

John Wesley shared a similar concern for a restrained adoration of the diverse qualities of God when discussing the three persons of the Trinity. By way of illustration, Wesley declared,

> You believe you have a *soul*. "Hold there," says the doctor; "I believe no such thing. If *you* have an immaterial soul, so have the brutes too." I will not quarrel with any that think they have: nay, I wish he could prove it: And surely I would rather allow *them* souls, than I would give up my own. In this I cordially concur in the sentiment of the honest Heathen, *Si erro, libenter erro; et me redarqui valde recusem*. "If I err, I err willingly; and I vehemently refuse to be convinced of it." And I trust most of those who do not believe a Trinity are of the same mind.[8]

Calvin, Wesley, and others were constrained to be explicit in their affirmation of the Trinity. They were concerned to hold a sufficient belief in the one eternal God but not an exaggerated or speculative affirmation. Evangelicals assume a unity of the three persons of the Trinity.

In affirming Father, Son, and Holy Spirit as a unity or godhead, one affirms their unique personhood as well as their work. For example, one speaks of the person and work of Christ. *Person* refers to the essential identity of Christ that is unchanging. *Work* refers to what Jesus Christ did and continues to do. These terms apply to all three manifestations of the Trinity.

To conceive of God as Father or a sovereign Ruler evokes a negative reaction among many. They associate a sovereign with oppression, a monarchy, a repressive tyrant. Others frequently tie God's providence to an unrelenting predestinarianism and human passivity.

Thorough biblical study, however, suggests a different understanding of God's sovereignty and providence. "Sovereign" suggests a ruler who is in charge. The evangelical affirms that God is sovereign, but not as a tyrant. God is simply "in charge." Support and encouragement for this view come from John Calvin's teaching about God's providence.

God provides. God makes provision for things needed but not necessarily for things desired.

In our day we see a resistance to gratitude or openly acknowledged dependence on spouse, parent, or child, let alone on deity. The illusion that haunts so many is that they are self-sufficient. People don't want to need anything permanently. So-called affluence and expanding gross-national-product figures suggest that the secular optimism about human self-sufficiency is well founded. But in the final measure, God provides something far more essential than affluence and self-sufficient energy resources. God provides salvation for all who are in Christ.

Titles for God like *Sovereign* and *Provider* refer to specific ways in which God relates to creation. God ultimately controls; God ultimately provides. God undergirds, picks up, and draws to Himself all activities through His sovereignty and providence.

One may employ the image of a mother hen gathering chicks under her wings to suggest God's caring sovereignty. The chicks hatch from the eggs that came from the hen's body and were incubated by her; hers is a sovereign and providential activity in the process that culminates in the emergence of the chicks from their shells. The mother's care for the brood after hatching suggests a continuing concern for the life of the chicks. This caring dimension in God complements His ruling sovereignty. God the Father relates to us through control and freedom, through transcendence and immanence, through creation and caring. In the current vernacular, we may express the sovereignty of God with the phrase "Hang loose, baby." God offers a covenant bond that invites one to be less anxious about tomorrow: "Everything will be all right in the end." Whatever or whoever oppresses, destroys, and blasphemes will be overcome. The old creation is becoming a new creation under the work and person of God the Father.

The sovereign God is the God who lovingly gathers the

world into final righteousness through the outworking of His righteous wrath against all that is evil (Matt. 23:37).

The second person of the Trinity is Jesus Christ. Historically, Christianity affirms the preeminent revelation of the Godhead in the Son, the historical person Jesus of Nazareth. The doctrine of the Incarnation (entering into flesh) teaches that God is person in the Son, Jesus.

Jesus was the healer, the minister. He suffered and died and was raised from the dead; He ascended and will return as mediator for those who by faith in Him participate in the new covenant. The church historically has affirmed the work of Jesus as the Son with the title *Christ*. Jesus is the Christ because of who He is and what He has done. The phrase *Jesus Christ* is an abbreviated confession of faith and not merely the first and middle name of Jesus Christ of Nazareth. Rather, these two names declare that Jesus is Christ: He is the incarnation of the Triune God (John 1:1–18).[9]

In Jesus of Nazareth one affirms the incarnation of God and the redemptive act on the cross by which we are saved from our sin. The sovereign God became enfleshed in the person of Jesus of Nazareth. God the Son is Jesus the Christ. *Jesus* and *Christ* refer to different dimensions of that one person.

The third person of the Trinity is the Holy Spirit. Affirming the person and the work of the Holy Spirit is essential for the evangelical. Many Christians hold a view of the Holy Spirit that is far too limited. God's Holy Spirit is the Comforter. The Spirit is the one whom Jesus promised to His followers (John 14:16–17). The Holy Spirit comforts, sustains, and empowers Christians for witness and service (Acts 1–2).

In addition to the Pentecost experience and the fresh outpouring of God's Spirit on the New Testament church, the Holy Spirit has always been active in creation, revelation, and redemption. This larger work of the Spirit necessarily encompasses the corporate and social activities of God often neglected by evangelicals. Such neglect is unscriptural and therefore reflects poor doctrine and deficient living.

The Holy Spirit convicts and woos the sinner in order for him to experience the new birth in Jesus Christ. This intimate and personal activity of the Spirit occurs in the life of each believer. The Spirit also works in the total life of the universal church, the kingdom of God. The corporate and catholic dimension of the work of the Holy Spirit is gratefully affirmed.

In sum, the tri-unity of the Father, the Son, and the Holy Spirit is a starting-point assumption, revealed in the Scriptures and in the faith of the believer and the church universal. We may think of the three persons of the Trinity as the three distinct ways in which God reveals and relates Himself to us.

A brief note is needed about the imagery used to describe the work and the persons of the Holy Trinity. Masculine images associated with Ruler, Messiah, and Sovereign are used to describe the work of God the Father and God the Son. Acts of comforting, supporting, and wooing may suggest feminine attributes in the work of God the Holy Spirit.

These images raise the issue of sexist language in evangelical theology. Evangelicals have an opportunity to be sensitive where language may have been overbearing, to be educated in matters where ignorance held sway. The matter of sexist language is a language problem per se; it is not essentially a theological problem. The emphasis of theological truths may have been in part misplaced by masculine language. But these misemphases cannot be corrected simply by changing the gender or "neuterizing" theology. Language is one issue; the theological truth behind the language is another issue. The use of "he/she" will not overcome the problem of failing to fully appreciate the reality of the Trinity.

The important question today is, In light of renewed cultural sensitivity, how does one reexamine the language of affirmations and testimonies of Christian experience and manage to retain the intent and perhaps strengthen the power of these affirmations by altering traditional language? Perhaps at certain points traditional affirmations of God the Father and God the Holy Spirit can utilize such words as *Sovereign, Providence, Ruler, Comforter,* and *King* and still remain faithful and sensitive to all concerned. But altering the language of the classic statements and creeds does not solve the problem of skepticism and unbelief.[10]

THE DISTINCTIONS IN THE GODHEAD

Wesley, Calvin, and others affirm the fact of the Trinity. They were equally firm in declaring the mystery that surrounds any

... three equal but distinct Persons ...

effort to understand the unity of the Godhead. Years of scholarly study and innumerable debates witness to the difficulty of an adequate comprehension of the Trinity as "three equal but distinct persons."

Less controversy arises over the fact of the three persons than the manner in which they are related. Some statements suggest an independence of the three persons that distracts from their unity in the Godhead. This subordinates one person to another. Other statements seem to force a unity. Here the three persons blur and their distinctive characteristics appear inconsequential.

Despite the difficulties in achieving an accurate balance, the church is called to affirm three equal but distinct persons of the Trinity. Calvin expressed it well:

> Now, although the heretics* rail at the word "person," or certain squeamish men† cry out against admitting a term fashioned

---

*(Footnote of J. T. McNeill, editor of *Institutes:*) Cf. sec. 2, note 6.

†(Footnote of J. T. McNeill, editor of *Institutes:*) "Morosi." If, as suggested in OS III. iii, Calvin had in mind here Bullinger's discussion of the two natures of Christ (*Utriusque in Christo naturae tam divinae quam humanae . . . assertio orthodoxa,* 1534), it is remarkable that no edition of the *Institutes* prior to 1559 bears this allusion. The 1536 edition associates *morositas* with the *heretici,* and in his *Response to the Questions of George*

by the human mind, they cannot shake our conviction that three are spoken of, each of which is entirely God, yet that there is not more than one God. What wickedness, then, it is to disapprove of words that explain nothing else than what is attested and sealed by Scripture.[11]

Part of the difficulty of interpretation lies in the ambiguity of language. Many of the words and concepts in Christian theology are Greek or Latin derivatives. Frequently words and their derivatives have very different meanings and a preferred meaning will have to be selected. For example, in discussing the nature of the Godhead, two Greek terms *hypostasis* ("essence") and *ousia* ("substance") may be used to refer to the three persons of the Triune God.

In general, both terms refer to that which underlies a thing, that which makes it what it is, its essence. In discussing the Father, the Son, and the Holy Spirit, theologians sometimes use these words in conflicting ways, as they may refer either to general or to particular characteristics.

The Latin translation for both *hypostasis* and *ousia* is the single term *substantia* ("substance"). The Latin *essentia* ("essence") was not used to translate either Greek word. In fact, *essentia* was not used in discussions about the Trinity. The Latin *substantia* therefore has had to carry the linguistic burden of affirming the unity, or oneness, of the Trinity. In Latin, *persona* ("person") is used to translate *hypostasis*. The Greek word *prosopon* ("person") is not used.

The next step is to examine the theological intention behind these words and concepts and to establish proper connections. The classic work *Documents of the Christian Church*, edited by Henry Bettenson, offers helpful assistance in this task. Consider his notes on *hypostasis* (ὑπόστασις):

Blandrata, 1557, Calvin applies to this anti-Trinitarian the adjective *morosus*, CR IX. 329. Cf. IV. i. 16, 20. It is certain, however, that Bullinger withheld approval from Calvin in the latter's dispute with Pierre Caroli, 1537. See Bullinger's letter to Oswald Myconius, July 23, 1537 (Herminjard, *Correspondence* IV. 264 f.; CR X. 2. 116f.; OS III. iii, note 4).

Used in two senses: (i) *General:* the essence shared by many particulars, as men, e.g., share a common ὑπόστασις of "manness" in virtue of which they are men; (ii) *Particular:* the essence of the individual, in virtue of which it is itself; almost "person." John Smith is John Smith because of an ὑπόστασις, "John Smithness."[12]

Bettenson's discussion suggests that the Latin word *persona* ("person") is approximate to the Greek *hypostasis.* This also means that the word *substance,* from the Latin *substantia,* will be used to refer to the essential unity, or oneness, of the Godhead.

The word *person* indicates an entity that has unique characteristics of its own, an identity. The identity, or *persona,* of an entity suggests that it has the capacity to integrate new experiences; it has personality.

This sense of vitality, the life principle of integrating new experiences, is more readily associated with personality than with substance or essence. "Character" or "presence" or "countenance" refers to the creative and integrative novelty of each individual; creative novelty suggests that an individual has personality, *persona.*

The word *substance* refers to a sharedness, a *hypostasis* or *ousia;* the Latin word *substantia* suggests a simple, undivided quality common in all the particulars.

In affirming three persons *(personae/hypostaseis)* of the Trinity, one affirms three manifestations of the Trinity. Likewise, an affirmation of the *substantia* of the Trinity declares that the manifestations, or persons, share a simple undivided unity, an equality in the Godhead.

Further discussion about the differences between person and essence would indulge the reader in an academic debate not relevant to the needs of this commentary. With no disrespect to the struggles in the early church, Calvin wrote:

Therefore, if the testimony of the apostle [Hebrews 1:3] obtains any credence, it follows that there are in God three hypostases. Since the Latins can express the same concept by the word

"person," to wrangle over this clear matter is undue squeamish-
ness and even obstinacy.[13]

Allow Calvin to point the way for us on this matter. In
passing, one is reminded that John Calvin was more absorbed
in writing about the doctrine of the Trinity than was John
Wesley. Certainly Wesley was not unconcerned about the
doctrine. He, like Calvin, affirmed the fact of the unity of the
Trinity and proceeded to the practical work of the gospel.

THE MYSTERY OF THE UNITY

Both Calvin and Wesley contribute to an evangelical understanding of the Trinity. For example, Wesley's sermon "On
the Trinity" serves as a guide
. . . mysteriously united in the God- in approaching the mystery of
head . . . the unity. In Wesley's thinking
there was no ambiguity or
mystery about the fact that the Holy Trinity was revealed in
Scripture. The mystery arises over how the Trinity is united.

Wesley observed, "Now the mystery does not lie in the
fact, but altogether in the *manner.*"[14] We all admit to a limited comprehension of the mysterious unity that is the
Godhead. But we do not need to be distracted by mystery to
the point that we believe in nothing unless it is absolutely
clear in our minds under all circumstances. Mystery does not
lie in the fact of the Trinity but in comprehending the nature
of the unity. And that is all right.

Wesley went so far as to claim that the Bible does not
require belief in "mystery." Requiring one to believe in mystery invites difficulties. That is to run the risk that mystery
itself, rather than God, becomes the object of faith. For the
Christian the core object of faith is not mystery but God.
Mystery surrounds the nature of the unity of the Trinity. But
this does not dilute the fact of the unity of the Godhead.

Those who fail to affirm the Trinity violate two theological
principles: (1) the unity of the Godhead and (2) the distinctive
personalities of the Father, Son, and Holy Spirit.

UNITY AND DIVERSITY

A firm belief in the Trinity keeps one from being drawn into the heresies of polytheism, manichaeism, and gnosticism. These deviations from God's revelation are introduced when the equality and the distinctiveness of the persons of the Trinity are not maintained. They are both ancient and modern heresies. The evangelical of today joins in the historic creeds to affirm the centrality of the Trinity against the polytheism, manichaeism, and gnosticism of all ages. To these ever present pressures to dilute the doctrine of the Trinity is added a fourth, Deism. The deist believes that God is Father, Creator, or Sovereign only. By assigning the power of God to initial creation, deism is the open door to universalism and unitarianism. Believing in God in a vague, general sense has been very influential in American theology. In effect the deist claims, "I believe in God in general, but don't bother me with any of the particulars." Many deists acknowledge some form of belief in God but are unwilling to accept the full teaching of Scripture. They don't believe in the redemptive work of Jesus or the sustaining presence of the Holy Spirit.

. . . which the Church historically has described as the Holy Trinity.

Another heresy is the insistence in a belief in Jesus only. This has been called Jesusism. Jesus is worshiped as "the God" of the Christian faith. Jesus is but one of three persons of the Trinity, not the only one. Jesus is the incarnation of God, but the Godhead is more than Jesus. Some would say, "Jesus only." This effort to acknowledge the reality of Jesus in one's life is perhaps well intended. But it is not enough. The evangelical cannot affirm Jesus as Lord and Savior apart from God the Father and God the Holy Spirit. A Jesus-only theology errs from Scripture and does not stand within historic affirmations of the church.

A third force that would dilute the historic doctrine of the Trinity is Spiritism. Many have experienced the work and person of the Holy Spirit in their lives. They have a compelling desire to glorify the Holy Spirit for spiritual gifts—speaking in tongues, healing, casting out demons. Spiritism is a lopsided emphasis on God the Holy Spirit and must be challenged inasmuch as it fails to affirm God the Father, God the Son, and God the Holy Spirit equally.

A wide range of theological options for understanding the unity and diversity of the Trinity has always been present in the church. But the evangelical endeavors to be faithful to both the Scriptures and tradition in affirming the three equal but distinct persons of the Trinity.

DISCUSSION QUESTIONS

1. Why is it important to believe in the Holy Trinity?

2. Does thinking of God the Father, God the Son, and God the Holy Spirit as persons make sense? Why? What warning must we bear in mind?

3. Is mystery a bad thing in our faith? Do we need to affirm mystery doctrinally?

4. Why is the doctrine of the unity of the Godhead essential for the scriptural Christian?

5. What happens when we "do our own thing" theologically?

6. Which of the three persons of the Trinity do you feel closest to? Why? Which person of the Trinity do you feel most distant from?

GOD
THE FATHER

Scriptural Christianity affirms that the first Person of the Holy Trinity, God the Father, is the Eternal One and reigns supremely. He has provided a covenant through which His creatures can be redeemed and through which His creation will be liberated from all evil and brought to final righteousness at the end of the age.

This chapter and the two that follow attempt to spell out the activities of the three persons of the Holy Trinity and tell why a delineation of the distinctive work and person of each of the three manifestations of the Godhead is essential for Wesleyan theology. Having focused on the formal relations of the persons of the Godhead in the previous chapter, attention is now called to God the Father.

THE INTEGRITY OF GOD

Evangelicals join the historic church in affirming the essential character and attributes of God. Wesley's sermon "The Unity of the Divine Being" is a helpful guide.[1] He declares that no one can search out God to perfection. "Only some of his attributes he hath been pleased to reveal to us in his word. Hence we learn that God is an eternal being."[2]

Scriptural Christianity affirms that the first Person of the Holy Trinity, God the Father, is the Eternal One . . .

Wesley lists six attributes that comprise the character of God. One is God's omnipresence. The Latin word *omni* means "all," and the word *presence* linked with it gives us a word that means God is everywhere and always present.

A second attribute is that God is "likewise all-perfect." His fullness and completeness transcend human capacity. Whatever we may conceive as perfection, God is that and more.

Another is God's omnipotence. Again, the word *omni* is linked with the Latin word *potent*, which means "powerful." God is all-powerful.

God is omniscient; that is, God is all-knowing. Whatever is to be known, God knows it.

Holiness is a further attribute. God "is light and in Him is no darkness at all."

And finally, God is Spirit. God, as Spirit, "called into being all that is." At the beginning of creation "the Spirit of God was hovering over the waters" (Gen. 1:2). God, the Spirit-Creator, is the one who created humanity in His own

46

image. The unique quality of humanity shared with God is what theologically we call the breath of life. This breath, or spirit, distinguishes human beings from the rest of creation. Thus, God the Father as Spirit creates the human spirit, or breath of life. God is the source of the human spirit.[3]

These attributes witness to God's eternal and transcendent nature. God the Father's eternal unity and completeness transcend human beings and whatever possibilities human beings might conceive for themselves or God.

THE SUPREMACY OF GOD

The phrase *reigns supremely* affirms how God relates to all that is less than God. Wesley conceived of God as Creator and Preserver: "The eternal, almighty, all-wise, all-gracious God is the Creator of heaven and earth. . . . He is the Preserver as well as the Creator of everything that exists." This affirms the immanence (involvement) of God in creation. Wesley put it like this: ". . . especially considering that nothing is distant from Him in whom we all live, and move, and have our being."[4]

. . . and reigns supremely.

This affirms the immanence of God in creation and His continuing creating and preserving presence. This God is eternal and omnipresent. One can affirm God's transcendence and immanence, His eternal being and His continuous participation in creation, as matters of fact. But "the manner of his presence no man can explain, nor, probably, any angel in heaven."[5]

Another aspect of God's supreme reign is self-imposed restraint. Because God is self-restrained in His supreme rule, we have free will, spontaneity, and the prospect of maturity in the faith as real possibilities. Of this self-restraining quality of God's providence, Wesley further noted: "If, therefore, God were thus to exert his power, there would certainly be no more vice: but it is equally certain, neither could there be any virtue in the world."[6] An absolute dependence on God would eliminate free will and the creative novelty that must exist for personality or individuality. An absolute dependence would, of course, eliminate any need for salvation as well. God would amount to little more than an intolerable tyrant under these circumstances.

God chooses self-restraint in His supreme rule. Thus God enhances Himself. Self-restraint does not damage the character of God, indeed God would not be God without self-restraint. Self-restraint is a gracious gesture. The spirit and potential for responsiveness to God that are in "the breath of life" are definitive characteristics of every human being. John Calvin too captured this measure of God's responsiveness. He claimed that the chief purpose of man, as expressed in the Westminster Catechism, is "to glorify God and enjoy Him forever." Human beings and other creatures are not totally disassociated from God. God's self-restraint is confirmed as His creatures respond to His grace in faithful praise and adoration.

God reigns, and His responsiveness in that rule does not diminish Him as God. Calvin supports this belief, saying that there is in God an "integral perfection."[7] At the end of the age, the eternal God who reigns supremely will surpass His previous relationship to creation; all creation will worship God. In his sermon "Spiritual Worship," Wesley shows the foundation needed for the sweet communion that the faithful have with God: The true God is intrically involved with the creation. This occurs because the branches are in the vine. "The true God," says Wesley, is "from eternity" and is "the sole Creator of all things." God is "the Supporter of all the things that he hath made"; He is "the Preserver of all things; . . . he is the true Author of all the *motion* that is in the universe."[8]

God is the redeemer and the governor of all things. God is the source, the Creator. God supports, preserves, invites, redeems, and encourages. The kingdom of God continues to unfold because God participates in that development. God is not diluted or diminished in this historical process of the becoming, or the coming, of the kingdom. God, the Eternal One, the Transcendent One, reigns supremely and is immanent in all. The scriptural Christian affirms these basic characteristics of God the Father, the being and becoming of God who reigns supremely.

THE COVENANT OF GOD

The phrase *He has provided a covenant* lays claim to the specific way by which God chooses to relate and to be related to as the Eternal One who reigns supremely. God provides or offers a covenant for humanity. *Covenant* means "arrangement" or "league." In a covenant one is in league with another. A covenant relationship claims that God offers a mutuality and a reciprocity to creation for communion, love, respect, and fellowship. This relationship is offered in Jesus Christ. The covenant occurs in

He has provided a covenant . . .   human history and therefore assumes the historical Jesus and the historical Israelites. A covenant must occur within the scope of history. It occurs within specific times and places. For the Christian, the preeminent covenant is in Jesus Christ and is expressed by the words "God so loved the world that he gave his one and only Son, that whoever believes in him shall not perish but have eternal life" (John 3:16). The only Son is the offer of a covenant relationship. In offering His Son for our sins, God has given, offered, or furnished a new covenant for us (cf. Jer. 31:31–34; Heb. 7:22).

The covenant is offered in the spirit of gracious love. The covenant relationship cannot be forced. Men and women are free to resist. God does not coerce, or force, one to believe, to enter into covenant relationship. The death of His only Son is a gracious offering for all who will believe.

The theological dynamics of the new covenant are suggested by John Calvin's statement under "the Knowledge of God the Creator":

Here let us observe that his eternity and his self-existence* are announced by that wonderful name twice repeated [Jehovah]. Thereupon his powers are mentioned, by which he is shown to us not as he is in himself, but as he is toward us;† so that this recognition of him consists more in living experience than in vain and high-flown speculation. Now we hear the same powers enumerated there that we have noted as shining in heaven and earth: kindness, goodness, mercy, justice, judgment, and truth. For power and might are contained under the title *Elohim.*[9]

THE GRACE OF GOD

The theological dynamics of the covenant relationships are this: "By grace you have been saved, through faith—and this not from yourselves" (Eph. 2:8) and "You are in Christ Jesus, who has become for us wisdom from God—that is, our righteousness, holiness and redemption" (1 Cor. 1:30). God expresses His love for us in providing a covenant of grace that all may be redeemed. Entry into this relationship with God is through faith in Jesus Christ.[10]

... through which His creatures can be redeemed ...

One experiences the covenantal offer of salvation as a social, corporate, and relational reality. Wesley makes clear that one enters a covenantal relationship by God's grace. God moves beyond the false religions of a religion of opinions, a religion of forms, a religion of works, or a religion of atheism.[11]

In contrast to all of this, Wesley asserted:

True religion is right tempers towards God and man. It is, in two words, gratitude and benevolence; gratitude to our Creator and supreme Benefactor, and benevolence to our fellow creatures. In other words, it is the loving God with all our heart, and our neighbour as ourselves.

---

*(Footnote of J. T. McNeill, editor of *Institutes*:) "καί αὐτουσίαν." Cf. I xiv. 3.

†(Footnote of J. T. McNeill, editor of *Institutes*:) Cf. I. ii. 2; III ii. 6.

> It is in consequence of our knowing God loves us, that we love
> him, and love our neighbour as ourselves.[12]

The covenant is historical, personal, and social. God's grace is not received if one attempts to exclude the neighbor or believes the neighbor is unrelated to one's own salvation and God's grace. There is no covenant apart from personal and social relationships; they are inseparable. The covenant is both social and personal, as God is both transcendent and immanent. The covenant is both immanent (personal) and transcendent (communal and social).

GOD'S LIBERATION OF CREATION

Human beings are the crowning act of creation. But the Christian is reminded of the *. . . and through which His creation will be liberated . . .* inseparable relationship of human beings and nature; all of creation is the subject of God's reign.

For example, Noah built the ark to save creation. This included representatives of all animal life as well as of humanity. God desires the redemption of all His creation.

The concept of a liberated creation is derived from Scripture (Gen. 3:17; Rom. 8:21). It reminds us that being created in God's image and animated by God's "breath of life" does not make human beings mysterious "spiritual beings," separate from and unlike the "material world." Everything is part of God's creative power.

THE RIGHTEOUSNESS OF GOD

God will free creation from evil in a final, complete, and perfect act. Deliverance, or *. . . from all evil and brought to final righteousness . . .* liberation, as a manifestation of God's righteousness is from all evil. God initiates this deliverance. Creation cannot bring itself to final righteousness but is brought by God to final righteousness. Creation itself is pas-

51

sive in this venture. God does the bringing. God is the source, energy, preserver, and redeemer. By God's power creation came to be. By that same divine power, creation will be brought into final righteousness.

Liberation from all evil is the movement to a final, complete righteousness. This affirms that original sin will at last be vanquished. A final and complete righteousness will replace it throughout eternity. Creation will then be restored to its position of original righteousness.

The doctrine of original righteousness affirms that in the beginning creation enjoyed a harmonious covenant relationship with God that was woven into the very fabric of creation and was without blemish. However, through the exercise of free will, mankind chose sin. A spontaneous yielding to temptation expressed the free will of Adam and Eve. Their choice did not spring from some fatal flaw in their original, essential character.

The scriptural Christian does not grant that original righteousness and original sin existed simultaneously. The term *original sin* refers to the first sin that occurred through exercise of free will. Original righteousness preceded original sin. The belief that all of creation will be brought to final righteousness affirms the hope that a final righteousness, akin to the original righteousness, will be established by God.

THE FINAL VICTORY OF GOD

One could use the phrase "at the end of human history" instead of "at the end of the age." Creation, as it is currently understood, may continue beyond the end of human existence. We don't know. We have no need to presume to know the final details. Neither is

. . . at the end of the age.

there need to assume or defend a premillennial, postmillennial, or amillennial anticipation of that end. What is needful is the affirmation that at the end of all time, God's righteousness will prevail: "Your kingdom come, your will be done on earth as it is in heaven" (Matt. 6:10).

DISCUSSION QUESTIONS

1. Why is it important to affirm that God the Father "reigns supremely"? Why, then, do evil forces have power in the universe? Is it too strong a statement about God the Father to say that He reigns supremely?

2. Scriptural Christianity affirms that God provides or offers a covenant and an opportunity for a right relationship with Him. Why do we affirm that God takes the initiative in these matters?

3. Do you believe that God's covenant extends to all creatures? Is redemption for all of creation? Why or why not?

4. Do you hold the hope of being freed, or liberated, from all evil at the end of the age?

5. What is final righteousness?

GOD
THE SON

Scriptural Christianity affirms that the second Person of the Holy Trinity, the Eternal Son, became incarnate as Mary's virgin-born Child, Jesus of Nazareth, the Christ. In His unique Person, He revealed to us both the fullness of deity and the fullness of humanity. By His life, suffering, death, resurrection and ascension He provided the only way of salvation. His sacrifice on the cross once and for all was to reconcile the Holy God and sinners, thus providing the only way of access to the Father. Now He intercedes as High Priest before the Father, awaiting the day when He will return to judge every person, living and dead, and to consummate His Kingdom.

The affirmation is simple and clear: God the Son is a person in the Godhead. This God became incarnate in Jesus of Nazareth. That God became human does not diminish the character of God. Rather, God is enriched through this action

Scriptural Christianity affirms that the second Person of the Holy Trinity, the Eternal Son, became incarnate . . .

because it is a profound gesture of grace by God on behalf of fallen humanity.

The word *incarnate* ("enfleshed") means that God took the form of human flesh in Jesus. Scripture clearly teaches this (Luke 1:35; John 1:14; Gal. 4:4; 1 John 4:2).

The Incarnation represents the ultimate in God's expression of love and humility. The title *Immanuel* applies to Christ. It means "God with us" (Matt. 1:23; cf. Isa. 7:14). This title is itself an abbreviated confession of the importance of God's becoming human in Jesus of Nazareth.

John Calvin's words are instructive at this point.

> On the other hand, we ought not to understand the statement that "the Word was made flesh" [John 1:14] in the sense that the Word was turned into flesh or confusedly mingled with flesh. Rather, it means that, because he chose for himself the virgin's womb as a temple in which to dwell, he who was the Son of God became the Son of man—not by confusion of substance, but by unity of person. For we affirm his divinity so joined and united with his humanity that each retains its distinctive nature unimpaired, and yet these two natures constitute one Christ.*[1]

---

*(Footnote of J. T. McNeill, editor of *Institutes*:) Throughout this chapter, as in the opening sentences, Calvin adheres strictly to the line of Chalcedonian orthodoxy. On this topic the study by J. S. Witte, "Die Christologie Calvins" in *Das Konzil von Chalkdeon*, ed. A. Grillmeier, III., 489-529, and W. Niesel, *The Theology of Calvin*, pp. 115ff., should be consulted. Cf. S. Cave, *The Doctrine of the Person of Christ*, pp. 151f.

THE MODE OF HIS INCARNATION

The question of the so-called virgin birth has been a center of controversy among Protestants

. . . as Mary's virgin-born Child . . .   for many years and for many reasons. It is necessary first to consider why the virgin birth of Jesus is affirmed and then to consider what is affirmed.

The word *as* means equivalent; therefore, the initial element in belief in the virgin birth is to affirm the earthly reality of the incarnation. The incarnation began with the conception of Jesus. The virgin birth is essential in affirming the incarnation of Jesus Christ, the Word become flesh.

The phrase "Mary's virgin-born Child" is preferred over "the virgin birth." Traditionally, Roman Catholicism has claimed the pure birth of Mary as well as that of Jesus. This is the doctrine of the Immaculate Conception. The Protestant claim is to affirm the purity of Jesus' birth only. Otherwise an indefinite regression is introduced.

Also, in this setting the word *Child* is preferred to *Son*. The theological emphasis is on the enfleshing of God, not sex identification. *Child* affirms all that is necessary without introducing distractions. There are two major reasons for belief in Jesus as Mary's virgin-born Child.

First, the Scriptures give witness to Jesus' virgin birth (Matt. 1:20; John 1:14; Gal. 4:4). Second, the affirmation is needed to establish proper teaching about Jesus Christ. The intention is to affirm the two natures of Jesus: He is fully God and fully man, truly man and truly God.

John Calvin affirms the virgin birth of Jesus in a theological context, and his witness may be our guide.

> For we make Christ free of all stain not just because he was
> begotten of his mother without copulation with man, but because
> he was sanctified by the Spirit that the generation might be pure
> and undefiled as would have been true before Adam's fall. And
> this remains for us an established fact: whenever Scripture calls
> our attention to the purity of Christ, it is to be understood of his

57

true human nature, for it would have been superfluous to say that God is pure.[2]

THE TWO NAMES OF THE INCARNATE SON

"Jesus of Nazareth" affirms both the humanity and the historicity of Jesus. The name *Jesus* [Hebrew, Joshua] means "The LORD [Yahweh] is salvation," or "The LORD is Savior."[3]

. . . Jesus of Nazareth, the Christ.

"Of Nazareth" anchors His life in its historic context. *Christ* is the messianic title given one anointed of God. Used together, these titles affirm the two natures of God the Son.

THE TWO NATURES OF THE INCARNATE SON

The nature of Jesus' birth supports the divine-human unity of Jesus, the Mediator. The uniqueness of Jesus' individuality and His historical personhood are affirmed. At the same time Jesus is the incarnate One, the initiator of God's new covenant, and the mediator between God and believers.

In His unique Person, He revealed to us both the fullness of deity and the fullness of humanity.

The traditional term *very* is not used because it fails to convey the sense of fullness and completeness in contemporary language. *Fullness* seems a better choice. The unity of the two natures of Jesus and the unity of the Godhead are affirmed, and that is what is important.

THE PROPHETIC FUNCTION OF THE INCARNATE SON

Protestant tradition affirms the work of Jesus in three theological functions: the prophetic function, the priestly function, and the kingly function. In the Old Testament, God used prophet, priest, and king to convey His grace and lordship. In Jesus the

By His life, suffering, death, resurrection and ascension He provided the only way of salvation.

three are united in the unity of His person and work. We affirm Jesus as equally Prophet, Priest, and King.

Those who share in scriptural Christianity affirm the historical existence of Jesus from His birth to His ascension. His ministry was filled with the particulars and specifics of service and with the prophetic declaration in His person that the kingdom of God "is at hand."

Some may emphasize Jesus' priestly function and neglect His prophetic service and witness. Calvin is helpful here:

> Yet his anointings as prophet and as priest have their place and must not be overlooked by us. Isaiah specifically mentions the former in these words: "The spirit of the Lord Jehovah is upon me, because Jehovah has anointed me to preach to the humble, . . . to bring healing to the brokenhearted, to proclaim liberation to the captives, . . . to proclaim the year of the Lord's good pleasure," etc. (Isa. 61:1–2; cf. Luke 4:18). We see that he was anointed by the Spirit to be herald and witness of the Father's grace. And that not in the common way—for he is distinguished from other teachers with a similar office.[4]

As Prophet, Jesus announced the coming of God's kingdom, performed miracles, and throughout his life, gave prophetic evidence that He was the Messiah who would reign supremely. The intent of His ministry was to provide access to the coming kingdom. In His prophetic ministry, Jesus pointed to the *only way of salvation* through His atoning death on the cross. He is the one way to God (John 14:6). This claim may appear exclusivistic to some; but in fact Scripture declares, and church tradition affirms, this is the plain truth of the matter. A complete statement of the theology concerning Christ as the only way of salvation will be developed in chapter 8.

An emphasis on the historical nature of Jesus' work needs to be accompanied by a warning. To be preoccupied with the historical details of Jesus can do damage to a full witness of the gospel. Caution is needed lest the proclamation that Jesus is Christ be argued solely from history and not from faith as well. Both are necessary. History and faith go hand-in-glove. Contemporary theologians Rudolf Bultmann and Karl Barth warn about belief in history only, and not in the work of Christ as well.

THE RECONCILING PRIEST

Here especially one finds assurance in the mediatorial action of Christ. Christ, as Mediator, stands fully and directly be-

His sacrifice on the cross once and for all was to reconcile the Holy God and sinners . . .

tween God and man, participating fully as the God-Man in both spheres, divine and human. In His unique person, Jesus is the only Mediator by which reconciliation between God and humanity may be accomplished.

This reconciliation is accomplished by the sacrifice of Jesus on the cross. To better appreciate the theological centrality and significance of that sacrifice, we turn to the words of John Calvin.

> The priestly office belongs to Christ alone because by the sacrifice of his death he blotted out our guilt and made satisfaction for our sins (Heb. 9:22). God's solemn oath, of which he "will not repent," warns us what a weighty matter this is: "You are a priest forever after the order of Melchizedek" (Ps. 110:4; cf. Heb. 5:6; 7:15). God undoubtedly willed in these words to ordain the principal point on which, he knew, our whole salvation turns. For as has been said, we or our prayers have no access to God unless Christ, as our High Priest, having washed away our sins, sanctifies us and obtains for us that grace from which the uncleanness of our transgressions and vices debars us. Thus we see that we must begin from the death of Christ in order that the efficacy and benefit of his priesthood may reach us.[5]

Calvin's language supports what is known as the satisfaction theory of atonement, also held by John and Charles Wesley. Other images or metaphors might guide our thinking about the sacrificial nature of the atonement. But the central teaching is that Christ's atonement was a historical event and that it occurred in order to reconcile God and mankind. Whatever sacrificial image or specific theory may be used to interpret this act of reconciliation, one must retain this reconciling and mediating function of Jesus. Some interpretations of 2 Corinthians 5:19 claim that Christ reconciled man to the Father's holy wrath. In this affirmation we want to clarify the positive intention of that language.

The reconciliation is mutual. God's wrath, or curse, closes off direct access to Him by unforgiven sinners. God's curse is set aside only through the work of Christ. Similarly, human pride, arrogance, and alienation are put aside. In Christ, the true Man and true God, God and man are thus brought to gracious reconciliation. That reconciliation is made possible in and through Christ Jesus alone.

THE EFFECTUAL PRIEST

Salvation is provided, offered, made available. But the evangelical believes that salvation becomes effectual only when it is accepted by a personal act of conscious belief, trust, and acceptance. The means of salvation was accomplished on the cross; but it is not effectual without the willing participation of the penitent sinner who confesses Jesus Christ as Lord and Savior and wills to begin a new life in Him. Christ provides but does not unconditionally guarantee salvation. Each person chooses to reject or accept Him and His work.

. . . thus providing the only way of access to the Father.

The emphasis on *the only way* underscores two essential theological dynamics: (1) Jesus' atoning work on the cross is the only way by which the righteous wrath of God can be set aside and (2) Jesus the Son is the only person who can provide that reconciliation and access to God.

Jesus reconciles the fallen world to the Father. God declares that His righteous anger and holy wrath are averted through Jesus Christ. Reconciliation occurs as the penitent

61

sinner confesses sins of pride, rebellion, alienation, and isolation. God accepts the repentance and extends forgiveness and personal acceptance. God begins to set aside, or repents of, His holy wrath and righteous anger by sending His only Son, Jesus. God initiates reconciliation in the birth and death of Christ; the prevenient grace of the Holy Spirit continues divine initiative and draws sinners toward acceptance of God's offer of salvation.

Philippians 2:6–8 indicates the majestic and humble manner in which Christ emptied Himself of transcendence and joined us by "taking the very nature of a servant, being made in human likeness" (v. 7). He became immanent in order to initiate reconciliation between God and humanity. Of all the events in the earthly ministry of Christ, the resurrection is of supreme significance. Christ was raised from the dead, thereby providing the only way of access to the Father, that we might be saved.

THE INTERCEDING PRIEST

Christ's atonement on the cross is central. But this did not complete His work. We would be premature to believe that Jesus completed His work when He ascended. As a person in the Godhead, the Son continues His work as heavenly intercessor for the believer. He completed the priestly function of reconciliation on the cross. Following His resurrection and ascension, however, Jesus continues His priestly function of intercession and will do so until His return.

Now He intercedes as High Priest before the Father . . .

Jesus is the great High Priest (Heb. 7:23–28). When we affirm Jesus as the High Priest, we also acknowledge and lay claim to the promise that all believers have direct access to God the Father through Jesus Christ the High Priest. No additional intermediaries or priests are needed to channel repentance and forgiveness in saving faith. "No one comes to the Father except through [Christ]" (John 14:6).

THE COMING KING

Jesus will return as the King, the Messiah, the Lord of Lords, the King of Kings. His return *... awaiting the day when He will return to judge every person, living and dead ...* is commonly known as the Second Coming, or the Parousia. Historically, this return has been called the "blessed hope" of Christians and the church.

The first coming is of course Jesus' birth in Bethlehem. The Second Coming is Jesus' return from the Father's right hand to judge every person, living and dead.

Generally the word *judge* has a negative flavor. A judge and judgment are associated with guilt and sin. However, the word *judge* also indicates the capacity for discernment between right and wrong, between good and evil. Thus *judge* and *judgment* should be clearly identified with the traits, motives, and activities that undergird honesty and fairness.

A judge should possess powers of discernment and perception that allow proper values to be assessed. In everyday experience, and certainly in theological experience, it is false to think of judgment in solely negative ways. In a measured and balanced way, the divine Judge discerns accurately the truth of each situation.

The clear result of judgment—however fair, honest, cautious, and discerning the judge and therefore his or her verdict—is a division. The case or issue before the judge ultimately is considered on its own merits. Judgment is inevitable in human experience, and certainly it is inevitable in divine experience. It is a just and fair division between good and bad, the just and the unjust. It divides those reconciled to the Father from those who remain unreconciled.

It is Christ, the Lamb, who will come to make the final judgment. This same Christ gave His life on the cross to provide access to God the Father. Those who have chosen rejection of that provision of reconciliation and those who

63

have chosen acceptance of that offer of reconciliation will be divided into two groups.

The final sorting out will be a separating of the wheat and the tares (weeds), the pure from the impure. In this judgment, God separates the unholy from the holy and thereby brings all of creation under His full authority.

THE REIGNING KING

Old and New Testament prophecies anticipate the coming Messiah, the return of Jesus Christ as Messiah and King. These prophecies carry an appeal: the imminent and eventual coming of the King calls for a decision to be made now. When the kingdom is gathered up *...and to consummate His Kingdom.* (consummated), one can be included in that historical social reality, the kingdom of God, if the decision to repent and make commitment to God's righteousness is made before one dies or before that event occurs. Thus, the call is always to believe *now*. Failure to decide for God is to decide against Him.

For the believer, Christ will bring to fullness and perfect completion the work that was begun at the point of creation by God the Father. The work continued in the sacrificial atonement of Jesus Christ is further provided through the work of the Holy Spirit acting with prevenient grace and it will finally be consummated in the kingdom itself.

God's kingdom is not a spiritual, mystical vapor. It is a corporate and historical reality. The kingdom is like an incarnation of the Holy Spirit. God's judgment will establish the kingdom of God in perfected form. The kingdom of God, prepared and delivered to Christ, may be seen as the fullness of the work of the Holy Spirit.

Accompanying the preparation of the kingdom is the prophetic function of proclamation that calls each of us to decide for the kingdom now before it is too late (Matt. 25:1–13).

In summary, God the Son has two natures: the one fully divine, the other fully human, so that Christ is both fully God and fully man. The work of Christ includes three functions: the prophetic, the priestly, and the kingly.

Whatever one's religious experience, the scriptural Christian affirms only one way for reconciliation between God the Father and the sinner. A new relationship begins when the believer is born again into a new relationship with the Godhead. That relationship continues and offers opportunity for maturity in Christ, who intercedes before God and who will return to consummate the relationship in the fullness of His kingdom.

DISCUSSION QUESTIONS

1. Do you see why we place strong emphasis on Jesus as the second person of the Holy Trinity?

2. How do you understand the belief in the virgin birth of Jesus of Nazareth? What are its theological value and limits? What are its testimonial value and limits?

3. Restate in your own words the doctrine of the fullness of deity and the fullness of humanity of Jesus Christ.

4. What is the *one way of salvation*?

5. What is the second coming of Christ? How is judgment related to the final consummation of the kingdom of God?

GOD
THE HOLY SPIRIT

Scriptural Christianity affirms that the third Person of the Holy Trinity, the Holy Spirit, was active from the beginning in creation, revelation and redemption. It was through His anointing that prophets received the Word of God, priests became intermediaries between God and His people, and kings were given ruling authority. The Spirit's presence and power, measured in the Old Testament, were found without measure in Jesus of Nazareth, the Anointed. The Spirit convicts and woos the lost, gives new birth to the penitent, and abides in the believer, perfecting holiness and empowering the Church to carry out Christ's mission in the world. He came to indwell His Church at Pentecost, enabling believers to yield fruit and endowing them with spiritual gifts according to His will. He bears witness to Christ and guides God's people into His truth. He inspired the Holy Scriptures, God's written Word, and continues to illuminate His people concerning His will and truth. His guidance is always in harmony with Christ and the truth as given in the Holy Scriptures.

THE HOLY SPIRIT IS GOD

The Holy Spirit has often been neglected as a person of the Trinity. Many believe that the Holy Spirit is little more than a vague spiritual blowing of the wind (cf. John 3:8). A basic mystery surrounds the person and work of the Holy Spirit; but specific affirmations based on the Scriptures, personal experience, and the writings of the Church are possible.

Scriptural Christianity affirms that the third Person of the Holy Trinity, the Holy Spirit . . .

In recent years, a dramatic reawakening and renewed awareness of the power of the Holy Spirit are in abundant evidence. Believers receive and practice the gifts of healing, speaking in tongues, and prophesying, for example. Such manifestations of the work of the Spirit are authentic, as they accord with Scripture's overall teaching. Hence, an extended statement about the Holy Spirit seems most appropriate.

THE SPIRIT IS FROM THE BEGINNING

For the Christian, Pentecost is the single most important demonstration of the work and person of the Spirit. The scriptural Christian, however, affirms the eternity of the Holy Spirit and the Spirit's participation from the beginning in all aspects and activities of the Godhead (Gen. 1:2). The ongoing creative, revelatory, and redemptive work of the Holy Spirit needs full acknowledgment.

. . . was active from the beginning in creation, revelation and redemption.

John Wesley readily affirmed the work of the Holy Spirit in creation.

> Our first parents [Adam and Eve] did enjoy the presence of the Holy Spirit; for they were created in the image and likeness of God, which was no other than his Spirit. By that he communicates himself to his creatures, and by that alone they can bear any likeness to him. It is, indeed, his life in them; and so properly

divine, that, upon this ground, angels and regenerate men are called his children.[1]

The Holy Spirit was present in the crowning act of creation—the giving of life to humanity. Whatever the Spirit's role in this supreme act of creation, it is comforting to know that He was actively present in all of creation.

THE SPIRIT ANOINTED PEOPLE FOR OFFICES

The three "holy offices" (those of prophet, priest, and king) were conferred on Jesus Christ in the New Testament period. Prophet, priest, and king are modes of God's revelation. The Holy Spirit anointed the prophet, the priest, and the king in the Old Testament period, conferring the power and authority of God's revelation on these figures. Hence, the Holy Spirit has always been active in God's revelatory and redemptive acts.

It was through His anointing that prophets received the Word of God, priests became intermediaries between God and His people, and kings were given ruling authority.

THE SPIRIT ANOINTED JESUS

The Godhead's creative, revelatory, and redemptive activity is clearly affirmed in both the Old and New Testaments. The Holy Spirit's power and presence is evident in the Old Testament and the New. The word *measured* means that God's power and authority were granted with limitation under the old covenant. The prophet could not act as priest or king. The authority of the priest could not be extended to include or usurp that of the prophet or the king. The authority of the king could not be extended to include that of the prophet or the priest. Power and authority were given to specific individuals and had specific limits. Ordinarily the prophet, the priest, and the king were three different

The Spirit's presence and power, measured in the Old Testament, were found without measure in Jesus of Nazareth, the Anointed.

69

persons with different purposes in their anointing.

But the power and authority given to Jesus of Nazareth included those of prophet, priest, and king. These separate anointings come together in Jesus of Nazareth, *the Anointed.* Jesus was anointed by the Holy Spirit to perform all these activities granted in limited measure to different persons in the Old Testament. These powers are without limit, without measure, without restriction in Jesus.

Jesus told His disciples about the revealing work of the Holy Spirit (John 16:12–15). He made it clear that the Holy Spirit would guide the believers into all truth because the Spirit would speak for God the Father and would illuminate Christ's ministry and resurrection victory.

THE SPIRIT WORKS IN REDEMPTION

Of the convicting work of the Holy Spirit, the writer of Hebrews observes that the Holy Spirit "judges the thoughts and attitudes of the heart" (that is,

The Spirit convicts and woos the lost, gives new birth to the penitent, and abides in the believer . . . of one's whole being) (Heb. 4:12). Nothing remains hidden from this ministry of the Holy Spirit. This discernment is the basis on which the sinner is convicted of sin by the Holy Spirit.

The curse of sin paralyzes conscious awareness of sin. One may live "comfortably" with sin, unaware of his or her sin and the need for a savior. But the Holy Spirit is already at work in that sinner's life, in the depths of the heart. The initial, or preparing, work of the Spirit moves the sinner toward a conscious conviction of sin. Apart from this preparing grace, or "prevenient grace," the sinner is unable to achieve any sense of wrong or sin.

In prevenient grace, as in redemptive grace, God takes the gracious initiative to save. This initiative begins as the Holy Spirit moves to soften the hardened heart. The softening process is a gentle movement toward conviction of one's sin.

As conviction deepens, the Holy Spirit woos the sinner toward repentance and redeeming grace.

Having been convicted and wooed by God's grace through the Holy Spirit, the penitent sinner is offered the new birth. The new birth is a gift. It is not merited; nor is it a just desert. Simply, it is a new life given in the death and resurrection of Jesus Christ. "Therefore, there is now no condemnation for those who are in Christ Jesus" (Rom. 8:1). There is no condemnation! There is new birth for the penitent. This is the heart of the Christian experience, and all Christian theology flows from this experience.

God's initiative is to be received by the penitent sinner as sins are forsaken. Peter's sermon to the New Testament church proclaims the truth that repentance precedes being born again: "God exalted him [Jesus] to his own right hand as Prince and Savior that he might give repentance and forgiveness of sins to Israel. We are witnesses of these things, and so is the Holy Spirit, whom God has given to those who obey him" (Acts 5:31-32).

Calvin, too, acknowledged the importance of repentance:

> Even though we have taught in part how faith possesses Christ, and how through it we enjoy his benefits, this would still remain obscure if we did not add an explanation of the effects we feel. With good reason, the sum of the gospel is held to consist in repentence and forgiveness of sins (Luke 24:47; Acts 5:31). Any discussion of faith, therefore, that omitted these two topics would be barren and mutilated and well-nigh useless. Now, both repentance and forgiveness of sins—that is, newness of life and free reconciliation—are conferred on us by Christ, and both are attained by us through faith.[2]

To be saved, or born again, necessarily includes: (1) confession and (2) acceptance of forgiveness. If we confess our sins to Christ, forgiveness is assured. Forgiveness is more than the willingness to forgive ourselves. First comes the fact that God has forgiven all who meet His conditions. As Wesley said after his own conversion, "I felt I did trust in Christ,

Christ alone for salvation."[3] When God's forgiveness is fully received, the believer ceases to carry guilty burdens and finds sweet repose in the sustaining presence of the Holy Spirit. In this fellowship the gifts of the Spirit are given and received.

THE SPIRIT DISCIPLINES

The notion of perfecting holiness enjoys little currency in the contemporary culture and church. Approximating the biblical notion of perfecting holiness is the general term *discipline,* or *discipleship.*

. . . perfecting holinesss and empowering the Church to carry out Christ's mission in the world.

Perfecting holiness means becoming more godlike, and this is a transforming work by the Spirit. The weaker terms *discipline* and *discipleship* could apply to anyone willing to accept discipline. Discipline may apply to the athlete, the successful housekeeper, the foreman, or the corporate executive. In fact, it is needed by anyone desiring to do well. For obvious reasons the classic term *perfecting holiness* is preferred. In this section it is used interchangeably with discipline, but perfecting holiness is the stronger term.

In Jesus' prayer for the church, He spoke of the perfecting and disciplining work of the Holy Spirit: "Sanctify them by the truth; your word is truth. As you sent me into the world, I have sent them into the world. For them I sanctify myself, that they too may be truly sanctified" (John 17:17-19).

The Spirit of truth is promised to the believer. The Spirit continues in the convicting, chiding, and wooing grace in order to move the believer toward continual repentance and good works in all of life. There is a continuing need for forgiveness in the perfecting of holiness and in the development of discipline among the faithful.

The Holy Spirit's ministry of perfecting holiness is captured momentarily in Wesley's sermon "Scriptural Christianity." He says:

Without busying ourselves, then, in curious, needless inquiries, touching those *extraordinary* gifts of the Spirit, let us take a nearer view of these his *ordinary* fruits, which we are assured will remain throughout all ages;—of that great work of God among the children of men, which we are used to express by one word, Christianity; not as it implies a set of opinions, a system of doctrines, but as it refers to men's hearts and lives. And this Christianity it may be useful to consider under three distinct views:

I. As beginning to exist in individuals;
II. As spreading from one to another;
III. As covering the earth.[4]

Perfecting holiness is not granted exclusively in extraordinary gifts nor in individual piety. The root of holiness is obedience; the fruit is the gifts that the Spirit bestows on the obedient. The statement affirms that the general work of the Holy Spirit is the ordinary fruit of holiness and discipline; added to this are special spiritual gifts. Perfecting holiness proceeds from an individual relationship with God outward—toward the group, toward society, toward the entire world. Holiness surely begins with individual lives yielded to Jesus Christ as Savior and Lord. But one's holiness, or growth in the Spirit, does not exist apart from the group and the society.

For example, Wesley's Methodist societies were instituted to encourage Christians to examine their maturity in godliness and to receive examination by peers in the small-group encounter setting. The discipline and the support of the group provided an ideal seedbed for God to effect the perfecting of the Christian life. These group examinations of a participant's walk with God encouraged discipline, stimulated confession, extended forgiveness, and generally provided mutual support, helping the members to give each other cheer and comfort in Christ. A dynamic church grew out of the disciplined holy lives of committed classes, bands, and societies. The aggregate effect of true individual holiness (godliness) is enormous corporate power. Conversely, corporate weakness is suggested by the lack of a proper godliness among believers.

The Holy Spirit, in perfecting holiness, brings God near. In his sermon "On the Holy Spirit," Wesley declared:

> For now we obtain but some part of his Spirit, to model and fit us for incorruption, that we may, by degrees, be accustomed to receive and carry God within us; and, therefore, the Apostle calls it, "the earnest of the Spirit;" that is, a part of that honour which is promised us by the Lord.[5]

Truly, perfecting holiness is an evidence that the Holy Spirit allows believers to carry God within (Gal. 2:20). Becoming like Him is for a specific purpose and ministry. Holiness is not to be used selfishly, to promote private pride and advantage, or to act without individual and corporate discipline. Discipline and true holiness are inseparable. Neither individuals nor the church are empowered to act without discipline or guidelines. Proper discipline always moves toward perfecting holiness, that is, walking as Christ walked.

The evangelical emphasizes the corporate dimension of the disciplined, the missionary intention of the believer being perfected in holiness, and the church that provides an environment conducive to facilitating godliness. As a corporate entity, the church and the constituent believers are perfected and empowered to carry out Christ's mission. "That God was reconciling the world to himself in Christ, not counting men's sins against them. And he has committed to us the message of reconciliation" (2 Cor. 5:19).

The purpose and the future of the believer and the church are that they may be perfected in holiness and power.

THE SPIRIT INDWELLS THE CHURCH

This chapter was introduced by a claim for the importance of the Holy Spirit's activity from the beginning in creation, revelation, and redemption. This stress on the continuing

He came to indwell His Church at Pentecost . . .

74

work and presence of the Holy Spirit does not distract from the uniqueness of the Holy Spirit's special work at Pentecost. Following Christ's ascension, the first special work of the Holy Spirit was the indwelling power given to the believers at Pentecost (Acts 2).

THE SPIRIT GIVES GIFTS

In recognizing the Spirit's work of granting spiritual gifts to the believer, we must stress the purposeful intent of those gifts. The gift of the new birth and the spiritual gifts are for the purpose of glorifying God and enhancing the work of the Holy Spirit in furthering the kingdom of God.

. . . enabling believers to yield fruit and endowing them with spiritual gifts according to His will.

Tremendous power is given to and released by the believer through the specific, special, and unique gifts given by the Spirit. The gifts are given to enable the believer to yield fruit. Their purpose is to (1) upbuild the body of Christ and (2) vitalize the worship of God. The Holy Spirit controls the power, the gifts, the fruit, and the purpose of the indwelling. The gifts are not for fondling and public display. Instead, they are given for the specific purpose of discipline, of witness, of perfecting holiness, of upbuilding the body of Christ, and of promoting the worship of God. Otherwise the gifts may be withdrawn, the fruits may wither, and the purpose of the gifts may be obscured and forgotten.

THE SPIRIT GUIDES BELIEVERS

Another specific work of the Holy Spirit is to bear witness to Christ. The Holy Spirit points to Christ and the Godhead. Paul reminds us of this: "For you did not receive a spirit that makes you a slave again to fear, but you received the Spirit of sonship. And by him we cry, 'Abba! Father.' The Spirit him-

He bears witness to Christ and guides God's people into His truth.

self testifies with our spirit that we are God's children" (Rom. 8:15–16).

The truth into which the believer is continually guided is the fullness of the relationship he has through God in Jesus Christ. This fullness occurs—by way of reminder—through the Holy Spirit: (1) God offers grace, (2) reconciliation is provided by Jesus, (3) the sinner receives salvation, and (4) growth begins in the grace and knowledge of that believer as a child of God.

THE SPIRIT INSPIRED THE SCRIPTURES

The importance of affirming the inspiration of the Holy Scriptures as God's written Word requires a section all its own (see chapter 6). "Scripture" means something written. Holy Scriptures are those writings claimed to be endowed and empowered with divine truth and presence. For the Christian, that empowerment is accomplished both in the original writing and in contemporary reading

He inspired the Holy Scriptures, God's written Word . . . of the Scriptures. In an era of the multimedia of television, recordings, films, and radio, there is a declining ability to read and write well. Nevertheless, the unique importance of the written Word of God is affirmed. It is a dimension of the special work of the Holy Spirit often neglected. The centrality of the Spirit-inspired written Word abides for the believer.

THE SPIRIT ILLUMINATES FOR DISCERNMENT

In this life there is no final perfection of human understanding. The Holy Spirit continues

. . . and continues to illuminate His people concerning His will and truth. to illuminate the hearts and lives of believers to give them increased discernment about the Godhead's revelation, power, and presence.

The Christian depends on the steady, faithful illumination

of the Holy Spirit concerning God's will and truth. "Will" refers to God's desire, intention, purpose, and promise for individuals and the church both now and in the future. Truth refers to revealed events and principles that are affirmed by faith. God's will and truth require the Holy Spirit's guidance and illumination of believers to assist them in perceiving and participating fully in God's will.

THE SPIRIT AGREES WITH CHRIST AND THE SCRIPTURES

The Holy Spirit comforts, counsels, and supports the believer. Additionally, the Spirit provides direction and guidance, prodding and directing the Christian toward specific intentions and goals that God has established (cf. Eph. 2:10).

His guidance is always in harmony with Christ and the truth as given in the Holy Scriptures.

The Holy Spirit always works in harmony with Christ. This affirmation may seem to vary from traditional affirmations that understand the work of the Holy Spirit to proceed always in a subordinate manner from God the Father, then the Son, and finally from the Holy Spirit Himself. Traditional understandings hold that no illumination is provided, no insights given, no experience affirmed, no revelation declared or clarified apart from Jesus! All that the Holy Spirit does must proceed in subordinate fashion from Jesus.

However, God's Word reveals that the Holy Spirit is a unique person, united with but not derived from the Father and the Son. This affirms further that the Holy Spirit acts in harmony with Jesus Christ. But the witness and guidance of the Holy Spirit have their own autonomy in the Godhead. The Holy Spirit acts in harmony with Christ, to be sure. But He does not proceed from Christ. He is equal to the other two persons, or manifestations, of the Godhead.

The guidance of the Holy Spirit does not conflict with or violate the person and work of Jesus Christ. Neither does the Spirit conflict with or violate truth as given in the Holy Scriptures. The Holy Spirit's guidance is in harmony with Jesus Christ, the living Word, and with the Holy Scriptures, the written Word. The Spirit's gifts, witness, and guidance are the relational activities of the third person of the Godhead, the same Holy Spirit.

DISCUSSION QUESTIONS

1. List some of the activities and responsibilities of the Holy Spirit.

2. What is "prevenient grace"?

3. What is the most important function of the Holy Spirit? Why?

4. Do you think the Holy Spirit is equal to the other two persons of the Holy Trinity, God the Father and God the Son? How? Why?

5. What aspect of your experience makes you feel nearest to the Holy Spirit?

6. What is the Holy Spirit's role in sanctification?

HUMANITY

Scriptural Christianity affirms that man and woman are fashioned in the image of God and are different from all of God's other creatures. God intends that we should glorify Him and enjoy Him forever. Since the Fall of Adam the corruption of sin has pervaded every person and extended into social relationships, societal systems, and all creation. This corruption is so pervasive that we are not capable of positive response to God's offer of redemption, except by the prevenient, or preparing, grace of God. Only through the justifying, regenerating and sanctifying work of the Triune God can we be saved from the corruption of sin, become increasingly conformed to the image of Christ, and be restored to the relationships which God has intended for us.

THE IMAGE OF GOD

"The Doctrine of Man" is the heading that Christian theology has used traditionally for discussing the relationship of men and women to God. This is acceptable if one understands that *man* is a generic term. It refers to the species *Homo sapiens* that includes, obviously, both men and women. However, the term *humanity* seems more appropriate for communicating the theological truth of the unity and equality of men and women as a unique creation of God. For this reason *humanity* is preferred as the heading for this chapter.

Scriptural Christianity affirms that man and woman are fashioned in the image of God . . .

Men and women alike are fashioned in the image of God, as we read in Genesis 1:27:

> So God created man in his own image,
> in the image of God he created him;
> male and female he created them.

The distinctive characteristic of humanity is its similarity to the image, or character, of God.

God breathed into man and woman the breath of life. God's breath, or spirit, is the distinctive, unique quality about men and women.

The word *image* suggests kinship or likeness. *Image* suggests a definite resemblance between mankind and God. However, human beings are not God. The dependent relationship of humanity on God needs open acknowledgment. Humanity is created in the image and likeness of God. This does not mean, however, that men and women are duplicates of God.

Jesus Christ alone shares in the unity of the Godhead. He transcends humanity but still participates fully in humanity. Only in Christ and the Holy Spirit are the image and the reality of God inseparable.

UNIQUENESS

Human beings do not differ substantially from other beings physically. All are created be-

. . . and are different from all of God's other creatures.

ings. But humanity does differ from other creatures in that human beings alone have the special gift of the breath of life (Gen. 1–3).

THE PURPOSE OF HUMANITY

God's intention is that men and women should glorify and enjoy Him. Human beings are wonderfully and gloriously created beings, capable of glorifying and enjoying God

God intends that we should glorify Him and enjoy Him forever.

forever; and that needs to be affirmed. God's purpose in creation was to make men and women who would glorify and enjoy a holy presence and a personal relationship with God. This relationship is the source of true Christian joy.

CORRUPTION

The introduction to this chapter affirms the initial intimacy of

Since the Fall of Adam the corruption of sin has pervaded every person and extended into social relationships, societal systems, and all creation.

God and human beings. In this "original righteousness" man and woman, Adam and Eve, enjoyed a full relationship with God.

But the fall of Adam broke that original righteousness and the wonderful and glorious relationship between God and humanity. The apostle Paul says, "Therefore . . . sin entered the world through one man [Adam], and death through sin, and in this way death came to all men [an indication of a doctrine of original sin], because all sinned" (Rom. 5:12).

Adam's fall introduced sin and no one since has been free from that burden. By one man's action corruption thrust its way into the intimate relationship that Adam and Eve had enjoyed initially with God. Sin thereby penetrated all of creation, disturbing the balance of intimacy present when God saw that creation "was very good" (Gen. 1:31).

In his sermon on original sin, John Wesley put the problem in a straightforward manner:

> Now God saw that all this, the whole thereof, was evil;— contrary to moral rectitude; contrary to the nature of God, which necessarily includes all good; contrary to the divine will, the eternal standard of good and evil; contrary to the pure, holy image of God, wherein man was originally created, and wherein he stood when God, surveying the works of his hands, saw them all to be very good; contrary to justice, mercy, and truth, and to the essential relations which each man bore to his Creator and his fellow-creatures.
>
> But was there not good mingled with the evil? Was there not light intermixed with the darkness? No; none at all: "God saw that the whole imagination of the heart of man was only evil." It cannot indeed be denied, but many of them, perhaps all, had good motions put into their hearts; for the Spirit of God did then also "strive with man," if haply he might repent, more especially during the gracious reprieve, the hundred and twenty years, while the ark was preparing. But still "in his flesh dwelt no good thing;" all his nature was purely evil: It was wholly consistent with itself, and unmixed with anything of an opposite nature.
>
> However, it may still be matter of inquiry, "Was there no intermission of this evil? Were there no lucid intervals, wherein something good might be found in the heart of man?" We are not here to consider, what the grace of God might occasionally work in his soul; and, abstracted from this, we have no reason to believe, there was any intermission of that evil. For God, who "saw the whole imagination of the thoughts of his heart to be *only* evil," saw likewise, that it was always the same, that it "was only evil *continually*;" every year, every day, every hour, every moment. He never deviated into good.[1]

Adam and Eve were the prototype of humanity, and their action has been determinative for each person since. Through disobedience they corrupted the close and intimate relationship they had enjoyed with God. This corruption is pervasive

and permeates all of human life. Wesley viewed sin as pervasive ("*only* evil") and persistent ("was only evil *continually*").
Sin extends to all that is touched by the human spirit.

Of further concern for Wesley was the human capacity to
establish substitute relationships and believe them pure.
Wesley said, "We worship ourselves, when we pay that honor
to ourselves which is due to God only" because, he further
declares in the same sermon, "Satan has stamped his own
image on our heart in self-will also."[2]

The curse of original sin began with the disobedience that
broke the original, faithful relationship with God. Human initiative was substituted and worshiped, creating pride and arrogance. Imagining themselves to be free from God and self-
determining, Adam and Eve (humanity) chose not to walk by
faith alone but by their own devices and desires. In eating of
the forbidden fruit of the tree of the knowledge of good and
evil, humanity concluded that it knows what is good, proper,
and just. Failing to walk by faith alone is the daily propensity
and the curse of original sin.

Wesley believed in original sin. Humanity cannot save
itself. It cannot experience the grace of God apart from divine
initiative. Human life has been so thoroughly corrupted by sin
that no one can hope to limp into the kingdom on human
merit. One must trust solely in Jesus Christ for righteousness.
One does not experience God's grace and favor apart from the
faith relationship. Original sin is the human capacity to turn
aside from God and to construct false gods in the place of the
true and living God. This pervasive curse of original sin is not
limited to individual beings. It extends beyond each person,
corrupting all social relations, all societal systems, and all
creation. This evil that permeates all creation is a direct con-
sequence and evidence of the Fall (Rom. 1:18–32).

Adam and Eve enjoyed original righteousness, and they
had the responsibility to care for all creation. In their sin they
became unrighteous and defaulted on their God-given task.
As a result, all creation fell into a distorted, evil perversion of

what God had intended it to be. This pervasive distortion and unfaithfulness commonly expressed by historic Christianity as original sin includes each individual, every social relationship, and any network of relationships within created reality.

INCAPABILITY OF MAKING A POSITIVE RESPONSE

Human depravity and misdirection that well up as a result of the Fall are so extended that the original, inspired likeness to God and the pristine intimacy with the Lord of creation have perished.

This corruption is so pervasive that we are not capable of positive response to God's offer of redemption . . .

Only one hope exists amidst the propensity toward sin. It is found in the biblical promise that out of death and ashes God can create human beings anew in Christ. Humanity is not able to be faithful on its own initiative. Humanity cannot respond on its own. "Satan has stamped his own image on our heart in self-will also."[3]

Wesley detailed seven evidences that support the belief that "we are not capable of positive response." (1) The imagination of humanity is evil. (2) Daily experience betrays human insensitivity about the spiritual state of life. (3) There is no acquaintance, closeness, or intimacy with God; there is only self-concern. (4) Natural language reveals no more saving knowledge of God among humans than among the beasts of the field. (5) There is no love of God, no agape; only a selfish love. (6) There is no fear of God, no awesome, holy reverence. (7) Love of sensual appetites leads men and women to pursue only those gratifications that are immediate and sensual.[4]

For Wesley, these activities are further indications of human incapability to respond to God without divine gracious initiative.

The pervasive corruption of original sin is (1) a sin bequeathed (sin inherited and transmitted by and through humanity) and (2) a sin begotten (sin initiated and created by and through human activities). Sin presents itself in two guises:

that which is endowed and that which is initiated. This dual character of original sin prevents men and women from making a positive response to God's offer of redemption and fellowship.

Underneath, throughout, and alongside original sin, however, is God's continuing offer of redemption. One cannot overstate the importance, reality, and dynamics of original sin; at the same time, in the midst of that sin and in the ashes of original righteousness, comes God's offer of redemption in and through Jesus Christ.

CONVICTION

God is constantly at work in the midst of pervasive sin. Through the third person of the Trinity, God convicts, woos, prepares, and enables the sinner to turn in the "right direction"—toward God. The Holy Spirit empowers sinners to respond to the grace of God and His offer of redemption. Human beings are not capable of a positive response to God's offer of redemption "except by the prevenient, or preparing, grace of God" through the Holy Spirit.

. . . except by the prevenient, or preparing, grace of God.

We cannot turn from sin on our own. The sinner is convicted and wooed first by the Holy Spirit. The depths of sin, of our turning away from God, are so encompassing of the human spirit that we are utterly cut off from any effective possibility of turning toward God. We cannot offer repentance and receive forgiveness apart from the thoroughgoing work of the Holy Spirit. The abiding presence of original sin so permeates every fiber of human motivation and intentionality that nothing within the human heart would otherwise turn us toward God in repentance. Apart from the prevenient grace of God's Holy Spirit penetrating to the very depths of human intentionality, we do not experience any conscious sense of sin and guilt or the presence of God's grace.

In the Wesleyan tradition prevenient grace is the initial

stage of God's redeeming grace. Original sin, as humanity's original motivational "equipment," blocks any effective effort we might make to turn toward God's grace. Therefore, individuals do not simply decide to repent and be saved. In effect, God decides initially, not by forcing a decision against our will but by graciously working deep within the motivational wellsprings to enable us to recognize that anything at all is wrong in the first place.

A turning toward God then becomes possible. This turning represents a positive response to God's gracious offer of salvation. The initial stage of conviction, however, is effected by God through His grace at work in the subconscious and unconscious dimensions of life, in the ashes of original righteousness. Through this awakening from original sin, one becomes open to the grace freely offered in Jesus Christ. Restoration to close and uncorrupted relationship with God is thereby made possible.

The phrase "great awakening" refers specifically to those periods when there have been outpourings of responsiveness to God's prevenient grace. People have been awakened through the Holy Spirit to their sin and corruption and, having been awakened, have turned to God, repenting of their sin and receiving God's full, redeeming grace. The historic great awakenings have been those periods when God's prevenient grace was most effectively present as seen in the huge numbers of people who were stirred in their ashes of original righteousness to make a profession of faith.

CONFESSION

Only through the justifying, regenerating and sanctifying work of the Triune God can we be saved from the corruption of sin . . .

The triune God in the fullness of the deity—all persons and manifestations of the Godhead—is at work in a glorious program of redemption.

Only through the justifying, regenerating, and sanctifying work of God is salvation possible. There is but one way.

Through the prevenient work of His Holy Spirit, God begins to prepare the sinner for reconciliation and justification. The first step in God's divine initiative is prevenient grace. This step is needed to prepare the sinner for the second step—justification by faith. Christ alone justifies the sinner. Christ opens the way for a faithful relationship with God, making possible salvation and righteousness.

The third step in the justifying work of the Triune God is loving acceptance by God. In Christ, God forgives all! When forgiveness is accepted, the sinner enters a new relationship with God; he is justified, saved, born again, made righteous. In sum, the three steps in the justifying grace of the Triune God are: (1) the prevenient grace of the Holy Spirit, (2) the reconciling grace of Jesus Christ, and (3) the pardoning grace of God the Father that extends to all who accept the offer of salvation. Put together, these three graces constitute the justifying work of the Triune God. But justification is not the whole picture of salvation.

A second stage follows. It is the *regenerating* work of the Triune God. Following the new birth, the justified sinner enters a new relationship with God. This new relationship is not one of complete heavenly bliss and mature fellowship between the believer and God. In this phase of the Christian life, a reconstruction work of grace is underway. Traditionally, Wesleyan theology refers to this as regeneration. Here God takes those dead, cold ashes of original righteousness and begins a spiritual reconstruction program. Regeneration begins as the living Christ indwells the new believer to begin the long rebuilding of heart, mind, and body so that the human spirit of the new-born child of God begins to recapture the spirit and image of God.

Regeneration is the shaking and the rebuilding of the foundations. Jesus begins to restore these newly born in His name as children of God to truly be sons and daughters of the living God. Regeneration is the making new in the likeness of God.

The third dimension of full redemption is the *sanctifying* work of the Triune God. God encourages the believer toward the likeness of Christ in personal, social, and societal relationships—the self, the family, the small group, the church, the community, the nation, and the world. To sanctify is to make godlike, or holy. We call the maturing of Christians sanctification; and it comes both in crisis experiences and in the steady process of growing in grace and knowledge of the Lord Jesus Christ.

The Triune God justifies, regenerates, and sanctifies. All three activities blend to save fully from the corruption of sin. Salvation begins with justification, it is further accomplished in regeneration, and it continues in sanctification. The Christian works out his or her salvation "with fear and trembling" (Phil. 2:12) because ultimately the goal is possessing the holiness of God (cf. Matt. 5:48).

CONFORMITY

In Christ, God has created anew the image of humanity's original intention. The pilgrimage in faith is toward conformity with the image of Christ. Christ's holiness increasingly permeates every fiber of the believer—his intentions, body, emotions, and intellect. The Christian is called to participate as fully with God in the future as was God's intention at the origin of creation.

. . . become increasingly conformed to the image of Christ . . .

God's intention in both original and redeemed righteousness is clear: "He chose to give us birth through the word of truth, that we might be a kind of firstfruits of all he created" (James 1:18). God intends that humanity should be the crown of creation, having the closest, most intimate fellowship and relationship with Him. Of the process of being conformed to the image of Christ, Peter says, "You have been born again, not of perishable seed, but of imperishable, through the living and enduring word of God" (1 Peter 1:23).

Justification, regeneration, and sanctification are all acts of God's grace. Together they move one toward the image of Christ. The Christian has the power and therefore the possibility to live in harmony with God, under His lordship. But that harmony does not come all at once. It comes in stages of transformation—justification, regeneration, and sanctification.

Being conformed to the image of Christ involves discipline, devotion, and piety in terms of a continuing and reflective worship of God. Thomas 'a Kempis was a medieval Christian writer concerned that believers conform to the image of Christ in daily life. In his classic devotional, *The Imitation of Christ*, Thomas encourages us to move more fully toward the form, the shape, the likeness of Christ. Conformity with Christ, sanctification, the perfecting of holiness, has always been a central concern to all Christians. The apostle Paul said it at the very beginning of the Christian church: "Christ loved the church and gave himself up for her to make her holy, cleansing her by the washing with water through the word, and to present her to himself as a radiant church, without stain or wrinkle or any other blemish, but holy and blameless" (Eph. 5:25–27).

CLOSENESS

Through the justifying, regenerating, and sanctifying work of the Triune God, the dead ashes of human righteousness are quickened, made alive, and restored in Christ Jesus. Those qualities of daily fellowship with God originally intended to be permanent in the act of creation (Gen. 1–2) once *. . . and be restored to the relationships which God has intended for us.* again are realized in intimate fellowship with the heavenly Father. This is made possible because the grace of God restores Christians to that vital spiritual intimacy originally intended by God.

In this chapter stress has been placed on the pervasive

evil, the curse of original sin, and the inability of human nature apart from Jesus Christ to have fellowship with God. This theological truth must be accepted prior to claims for a sweet communion and a gentle, loving fellowship with God. As much as we human beings want to be loved, the possibility of a close, intimate fellowship with God begins with God's initiative, however, not with ours. We cannot move toward that grace on our own. God brings grace to us through the prevenient working of the Holy Spirit. That's how it begins. Next, God extends grace to us for reconstruction of our sinful lives through the atoning work of Jesus Christ. Finally, God offers grace to put on the final touches of perfection in our walk with the Lord. This is God's sanctifying work, moving us toward holiness in daily life.

Thus, the Triune God acts in three decisive ways to restore the mutually trusting and affirming relationship between the Godhead and humanity originally intended in creation but put off by original sin. It is in this hope and in this conformity that the Christian lives and moves toward a perfecting of love with God.

DISCUSSION QUESTIONS

1. What evidences do you observe that human beings "are different from all of God's other creatures"? Is this important in our day?

2. What is the importance of affirming (1) total depravity, (2) original righteousness, and (3) prevenient grace? Where does sin come from?

3. Do you believe that sin is both a personal and a social reality? Why or why not? Illustrate.

4. Can we save ourselves? List some ways we try and the results of these efforts.

5. Do you understand prevenient grace? Do you believe in it?

6. What is the threefold redemptive act by the Triune God? Is one element more important than the others? Can one element exist without the others?

7. How do we conform to the image of Christ?

THE
HOLY SCRIPTURES

Scriptural Christianity affirms as the only written Word of God the Old and New Testaments. These Holy Scriptures contain all that is necessary for our knowledge of God's holy and sovereign will, of Jesus Christ the only Redeemer, of our salvation, and of our growth in grace. They are to be received through the Holy Spirit as the guide and final authority for the faith and conduct of individuals and the doctrines and life of the Church. Whatever is not clearly revealed in, or plainly established as truth by, the Holy Scriptures cannot be required as an article of faith nor be taught as essential to salvation. Anything contrary to the teachings of the Holy Scriptures is contrary to the purposes of God and must, therefore, be opposed. The authority of Scripture derives from the fact that God, through His Spirit, inspired the authors, causing them to perceive God's truth and record it with accuracy. It is evident that the Holy Scriptures have been preserved during the long process of transmission through copyists and translators, and we attribute such accurate preservation to the work of the Holy Spirit. These Scriptures are supremely authoritative for the Church's teaching, preaching, witness, identifying error, correcting the erring, and training believers for ministry in and through the Church.

In previous sections the Godhead, humanity, and the interactions between them have been affirmed. In this section affirmation of the Bible and its truth and witness is made. Almost instinctively people respond quickly to affirm the truth and power of persons. But in an age so dominated by the electronic, nonprint media, the truth and power of the written word in everyday life is more difficult to affirm. The Bible, or any other book for that matter, may appear, in contrast to persons, to be of less value and contain less power to transform. But such is not the case. Scriptural Christianity—the theological trademark of the evangelical Christian, the orthodox believer—affirms that the Bible, God's written Word, is holy. It is inspired, and therefore is vibrant and alive; it is an abiding, living Word throughout the generations. God's revelatory Word historically has been affirmed in two forms: (1) God's incarnational revelation in Jesus Christ of Nazareth and (2) God's written revelation in the Scriptures of the Old and New Testaments.

Jesus is God's living Word. The Bible is God's written Word. The Bible is a dynamic witness and revelation of God's purpose. The Bible, however, is not more central for faith than is God's Son, Jesus the Christ. Some misunderstand this relationship and thereby depreciate the centrality of the Scriptures in God's revelation. This failure to affirm the power and authority of Scripture is seen where there is a preference for a "flat" theology of the Scripture that affirms only the secondary or "witness" function of the Scripture. But such a view is not oriented toward scriptural Christianity in which the Bible is affirmed as the unique and sole *source* of written revelation.

The person Jesus is not to be lifted out and above the Scripture as a source or kind of revelation totally different from God's written Word, the Bible. To do this suggests that God's revelation occurs on two different and basically unrelated planes of experience: a person and a text. Apart from God's abiding presence in Jesus and in the Scriptures, neither the man Jesus nor the written text of the Bible would be sufficient to effect salvation. Jesus, the Word, and the Bible, the Word, both are forms of one revelation.

Without the objective reference of Scripture, one's experience of Jesus can turn into anything, including Jesus worship; that is, worship of Jesus to the exclusion of worship of the Father and the Spirit. This is called Jesus-idolatry. The Bible is the written, objective, inspired Word of God and as such it restrains subjectivism, holding theological reins on a totally interior, experiential christology. The Scriptures and Jesus are inseparably related. All that can be known about Jesus authoritatively is found in the Scriptures. Apart from the Scriptures, there are only opinions to guide; there is no transcendent authority as a standard for truth.

God's special revelation occurs in Jesus, and the Scriptures are God's living guide for that revelation. Christ is the incarnate Word; the Holy Scriptures are the explanatory Word. They declare the incarnation in order that humanity may be fully and accurately introduced to, understand, and participate in Jesus, the incarnate Word. Scripture is fully trustworthy because "all Scripture is God-breathed, and is useful for teaching, rebuking, correcting and training in righteousness, so that the man of God may be thoroughly equipped for every good work" (2 Tim. 3:16, 17).

The Holy Scriptures appear to be more readily accessible than Jesus Christ. Therefore, a second error may become a wedge between Jesus and the Scriptures. This error is Bible-text worship, and it too is a form of idolatry. A printed page is easily touched or seen. Unless spiritual care is exercised, one can easily become preoccupied with a written page and forget the necessity of faithful worship of the Lord Jesus Christ. The sin of "worshiping" the Bible is called bibliolatry.

The balance of the living Word and the written Word is needed and affirmed in scriptural Christianity. Full participation in the life of the Scriptures directs one's Christian pilgrimage to more fully conform to the image of Christ through the illumination of the Holy Spirit. The "wrong" use of the Bible stands in the way of growing in "the grace and knowledge" of the Lord Jesus Christ.

THE BIBLE IS ABOUT GOD

The Holy Scriptures are principally by God and about God and God's relation to the world. The Holy Scriptures are not basically about human history or human progress or failure. The Bible is about God's divine initiative in history. Therefore the proper use of the Scriptures is suggested by the three functions that the Bible provides for the believers.

1. *Referential.* The Scriptures are a source one must refer to for correct understanding about the nature and activities of the Godhead. This includes, of course, the whole sweep of the Scriptures, beginning in the Book of Genesis and going on through to Revelation.

2. *Intentional.* The Scriptures reveal the intention and will of God toward humanity and all creation. That intention is revealed as it is in history, as it is now occurring, and as it will happen. Especially important is the role of the Scriptures in setting forth God's plan of redemption that centers in Jesus Christ.

3. *Devotional.* The Scriptures are the basic authority for the devotional, worship, and liturgical life of the believer. The Bible is the primary resource for faith and for discernment of God's purpose now, as well as historically in retrospect and prophetically into the future. The Bible is also a means by which believers, both individually and corporately, commune with God and strive for faithful obedience in daily life.

The purpose of the Scriptures is to reveal God's activities, God's plan, and God's glory so that Christians may enjoy His glory, majesty, and presence forever. Consider John Wesley's Articles of Religion, "Article V. *Of the Sufficiency of the Holy Scriptures for Salvation.*" It is a sound guide.

> The Holy Scripture containeth all things necessary to salvation; so that whatsoever is not read therein, nor may be proved

thereby, is not to be required of any man that it should be believed as an article of faith, or be thought requisite or necessary to salvation. In the name of the Holy Scripture we do understand those canonical books of the Old and New Testament of whose authority was never any doubt in the Church. . . ."[1]

Therefore, along with Jesus Christ, the Scriptures stand above all other authorities and resources for the faithful Christian life. Clearly in matters of revelation the Scriptures stand above human experience to inform and form the teaching and hermeneutical task of the church. We are servants of the Word of God; we are not its masters.

THE ONLY WRITTEN WORD OF GOD

This phrase affirms the canon of the Holy Scriptures, a total of sixty-six books, thirty-nine constituting the Old Testament, and twenty-seven the New Testament. This statement clarifies the boundaries of Holy Writ.

Scriptural Christianity affirms as the only written Word of God the Old and New Testaments.

Further, it is essential in Wesleyan theology to acknowledge that the written Word of God and its authority come from God. That authority and power do not come from any other source, whether a church, a denomination, a council, or an individual. The authority of Scripture is from God and none other. In his *Institutes* Calvin speaks directly to the issue:

Before I go any further, it is worth-while to say something about the authority of Scripture,* not only to prepare our hearts to

---

*(Footnote by John T. McNeill, editor of *Institutes*:) Chapters vii–ix form an excursus on Biblical authority. Both the doctrines of the deity of the Spirit (I. xiii. 14–15) and the redemptive work of the Spirit (Book III, throughout, especially chs. i–ii) form the immediate theological context of the doctrine of the "inner testimony." Calvin refers the reader "elsewhere" (I. vii. 5), but this has often been overlooked. It is crucial for the interpretation of Calvin whether this doctrine of Scripture is seen as complete in itself

97

reverence it, but to banish all doubt. When that which is set forth is acknowledged to be the Word of God, there is no one so deplorably insolent—unless devoid also both of common sense and of humanity itself—as to dare impugn the credibility of Him who speaks. Now daily oracles are not sent from heaven, for it pleased the Lord to hallow his truth to everlasting remembrance in the Scriptures alone (cf. John 5:39). Hence the Scriptures obtain full authority among believers only when men regard them as having sprung from heaven, as if there the living words of God were heard.[2]

Accordingly, without the illumination of the Holy Spirit, the Word can do nothing. From this, also, it is clear that faith is much higher than human understanding.[3]

The affirming intention in Calvin's statement is to declare simply that the origin of the Scriptures is God. Calvin claims that by faith one is enabled to regard the words of the Scriptures "as having sprung from heaven, as if there the living words of God were heard." This reminds all that the source and the authority of the Scriptures is the Godhead, though writers recorded God's truth in their own expressive styles.

THE SCRIPTURES REVEAL NECESSARY TRUTHS

Scripture witnesses principally to the reality of the Godhead, the Holy Trinity, the Triune God. God's supreme power in creation—"God's holy and sovereign will"—testifies to God the Father.

These Holy Scriptures contain all that is necessary for our knowledge of God's holy and sovereign will, of Jesus Christ the only Redeemer, of our salvation, and of our growth in grace.

Secondly, the Scriptures point to the redemptive manifestation of the Godhead in the Son.

Thirdly, the Scriptures point to the sanctifying work of the Godhead in the kingdom of God which is manifest in the work of God the Holy Spirit.

---

or in the larger epistemological context of III. ii. Cf. Warfield, *Calvin and Calvinism*, p. 71, *et passim;* Doumergue, *Calvin* IV. 68, 247; Dowey, *The Knowledge of God in Calvin's Theology*, pp. 87, 157–164, 174.

Next a word about the phrase, "these Holy Scriptures contain." This positive statement should not be confused with a "low" view of Scripture that limits the authority of Scripture to the claim that "the Bible contains the Word of God." The Scriptures *are* the Word of God and therefore contain all the instruction necessary for salvation and the godly life. Therefore no further word of revelation or guidance is required; it remains only for the believer to live out the truth of God's Word become flesh. The Scriptures do not require supplemental readings to fully attest to the essentials of (1) a knowledge of God, (2) knowing Jesus Christ as Redeemer, (3) repentance and redemption, and (4) growth in the faith.

The Scriptures not only contain what is necessary for salvation but they also give clear and understandable focus to all that is necessary for the faithful life in Christ Jesus. John Calvin expresses the perspicuity, the essential focusing quality, of the Bible:

> Just as old or bleary-eyed men and those with weak vision, if you thrust before them a most beautiful volume, even if they recognize it to be some sort of writing, yet can scarcely construe two words, but with the aid of spectacles will begin to read distinctly; so Scripture, gathering up the otherwise confused knowledge of God in our minds, having dispersed our dullness, clearly shows us the true God.[4]

The Scriptures put into focus what is essential for a right relationship with God; a knowledge of God, of Jesus Christ as the only Redeemer, and of the dynamic process of salvation; and the perfecting of holiness in the believer.

INSPIRATION OF SCRIPTURE

The Scriptures contain all that is necessary for establishing a right relationship with God and neighbor. God's Word has been received and passed along through inspiration of the Holy Spirit in the Old and

They are to be received through the Holy Spirit as the guide and final authority for the faith and conduct of individuals and the doctrines and life of the Church.

New Testaments—and through the life of the church as the body of Christ to the present day. The Holy Spirit, the continuing presence of God, plows God's will and revelation into human understanding. The Holy Spirit provides continuity in the life of the Scriptures, both inspiring the original writing and illuminating the reading of God's Word. Use of the analytical tools available to the believer, under the prayerful guidance of the Holy Spirit, makes fuller access to the truth of the written Word of God possible. Calvin observed,

> At any rate, there is no doubt that firm certainty of doctrine was engraved in their hearts, so that they were convinced and understood that what they had learned proceeded from God.*[5]

Further, the inspiration and illumination of God the Holy Spirit establish the authority of the Word of God in the Christian's life. Of this power John Calvin claimed, "We ought to remember what I said a bit ago: credibility of doctrine is not established until we are persuaded beyond doubt that God is its Author.†[6]

Such persuasion is not the result of extended argument and hot debate. Persuasion that extends beyond doubt, according to Calvin, is this:

> The testimony of the Spirit is more excellent than all reason. For as God alone is a fit witness of himself in his Word,‡ so also the Word will not find acceptance in men's hearts before it is sealed by the inward testimony of the Spirit.[7]

---

*(Footnote of John T. McNeill, editor of *Institutes*:) Cf. II. vi, vii, and III, passim. On the covenant, see also II. viii. 21; II. x. 1–5, 8; II. xi. 4, 11; III. xvii. 6; III. xxi. 5–7; IV. xiv. 6; IV. xv. 22; IV. xvi. 5, 6, 14; IV. xvii. 20.

†(Footnote of J. T. McNeill, editor of *Institutes*:) Cf. Aquinas, *Summa Theol.* I. i. 10: "The Author of Holy Scripture is God."

‡(Footnote of J. T. McNeill, editor of *Institutes*:) Cf. Hilary of Poitiers, *On the Trinity* I. xviii: "For He whom we can know only through his own utterances is a fitting witness concerning himself" (MPL 10.38. tr. NPNF 2 ser. IX. 45).

The Holy Spirit convicts and woos the lost in matters essential for salvation; the Holy Spirit convicts and woos in matters of reason and understanding. The Holy Spirit prepares one to receive initial salvation and inspires the Christian and the church to a fullness of faith and conduct. Without this preparing witness of the Holy Spirit, salvation and the authority of Scripture slip beyond the reasonable grasp of men and women.

> Therefore, if faith turns away even in the slightest degree from this goal toward which it should aim, it does not keep its own nature, but becomes uncertain credulity and vague error of mind. The same Word is the basis whereby faith is supported and sustained; if it turns away from the Word, it falls. Therefore, take away the Word and no faith will then remain.[8]

Devoted study is necessary for full and proper faith and proper conduct in the church. The oft-noted diminution of the authority of the Scriptures in matters of faith and practice within the church nowadays is the failure of an active, engaging study of the Word of God. Yet it is an inescapable and disturbing fact of the day that many people, clergy and laity alike, are uncomfortable when they engage themselves in fervent study of the Bible. Calvin succinctly points to the importance of the Scriptures in faith and practice. He suggests what is lost in meager or undisciplined study of the Scriptures:

> Now, in order that true religion may shine upon us, we ought to hold that it must take its beginning from heavenly doctrine and that no one can get even the slightest taste of right and sound doctrine unless he be a pupil of Scripture. Hence, there also emerges the beginning of true understanding when we reverently embrace what it pleases God there to the witness of himself. But not only faith, perfect and in every way complete, but all right knowledge of God is born of obedience.* And surely in this re-

---

*(Footnote of J. T. McNeill, editor of *Institutes*:) This sentence, *"Omnis recta cognitio Dei ab obedientia nascitur,"* is quoted by K. Barth in affirming that dogmatics must presuppose Christian faith (*Kirchliche Dogmatik* I. i. 17; tr. G. T. Thomson. *The Doctrine of the Word of God* I. 19).

spect God has, by his singular providence, taken thought for mortals through all ages.[9]

The "singular providence" to which Calvin alludes is the affirmation that "the Word of God as Holy Scripture" is essential to feed and nurture the believer in the faith and practice of Christianity. The Holy Scriptures are to be received from the church and illuminated by the Holy Spirit. The partnership of the church as the "living magisterium" and the Holy Spirit as the "living inspiration" of the Trinity form final interpretive authority for the use and reading of the Bible. The final authority in matters of faith and practice in the church is the Holy Scripture accompanied by the indwelling presence of God's Holy Spirit. It is the Spirit who guides the church and believers into all truth. All individuals and the ecclesial community or the communion of believers come under the authority of the Scriptures. The believing community does not supersede or transcend the "supernatural" authority of God's Word, illuminated by the Holy Spirit, who guides in matters of faith and practice. Likewise the authority of the Scriptures and the presence of the Spirit transcend the Christian. Neither the individual believer nor the corporate community of believers transcends the Word of God, the Holy Scripture.

The witness and authority of the Scriptures are given for faith (that which pertains to salvation) and for conduct (that which pertains to obeying God). Faith and good works are inseparable in the Christian experience. Scripture guides in salvation and in good works and remains the rightful final authority (Eph. 2:8–10). Ultimately, the believer is under the authority of Scripture. Scripture is our divine guide. It is also the guide for the life of the church in all spiritual matters: (1) faithful teaching, (2) faithful obedience, (3) faithful witness, and (4) faithful fellowship.

THE EXCLUSIVE AUTHORITY OF SCRIPTURE

The Word of God preeminently bears witness and persuades of the salvation that is available to all in Christ. There are no

Whatever is not clearly revealed in, or plainly established as truth by, the Holy Scriptures cannot be required as an article of faith nor be taught as essential to salvation.

further authorities by which the essentials for salvation are established.

The contrasting phrases "clearly revealed in" and "plainly established as truth by" are a witness to the dual character of the Scriptures. The first phrase, "clearly revealed in," pertains to God's direct revelation in the Bible. Any person who wishes salvation can open the Bible and read it profitably without benefit of commentary, preaching, leader-directed Bible study, discussion, and/or prayer group. The Holy Spirit provides sufficient instruction through illumination for salvation.

The second phrase, "plainly established as truth by," affirms truths that are not immediately apparent at first reading. A thorough, disciplined study of the Scriptures aided by careful analyses of biblical passages enables the believer to perceive God's truth as plainly established. In practical terms, the evangelical finds clearly revealed truth in a reverent and thoughtful reading of the Bible. A second level of truth that guides in matters beyond salvation-truth is the distilled truth in which the further will of God is discerned. Both types of scriptural truth are necessary in establishing and teaching what is essential for salvation and growth in faith.

CONTRARY TEACHING TO BE OPPOSED

This statement underscores the theological truth expressed by the preceding statement. It affirms the limits of theological truth. The purpose of each statement is to clarify the authority of the Scriptures as they bear witness to, teach, and reveal what is essential for salvation. This present statement declares

Anything contrary to the teachings of the Holy Scriptures is contrary to the purposes of God and must, therefore, be opposed.

that anything that would add to or detract from what God's Word teaches in the dual character of its proper authority must be opposed. What is

103

the clear and perceived revelation of the Scriptures is both essential and sufficient for salvation. The Bible establishes boundaries for acceptable belief. Anything that would directly oppose the teachings of Holy Scripture is to be opposed on theological not preferential grounds.

This needed caution about the place of the Scriptures is not registered to oppose the use of Bible commentaries or study guides, nor should it be appealed to as a basis for thrusting aside the general wisdom conveyed through culture in general. Study aids and accumulated wisdom may indeed enhance understanding of the truths of God's Word. Nevertheless, these are merely tools or aids in studying the Bible and are not authoritative in themselves. They complement the Scriptures in matters of faith and practice. But they do not take precedence over the Scriptures. (See the discussion on hermeneutical methodology at the end of this chapter, pp. 109–19.) The Holy Spirit engages each individual in effectual reading of the Bible. A study of the Scriptures unaccompanied by the leading of the Holy Spirit is without spiritual, salvific benefit.

DIVINE AND HUMAN AUTHORSHIP

Because the Scriptures are the Word of God, they are the final authority in matters of faith and conduct (doctrine and life). This authority is established by God's intention in the original giving of the Scriptures, both oral and written.

The authority of Scripture derives from the fact that God, through His Spirit, inspired the authors. . . .

The initial or primary phase by which God established the Scriptures derives from their inspired authority. God's inspiring of the Scriptures is a continuing phenomenon, similar to creation. Inspiration extends beyond God's initial guidance in receiving and recording the Word. Inspiration also includes the accurate preservation of God's Word in speech and script, and the abiding power of the Scriptures to inspire authentic teaching and preaching in the general ministries of Christ's church.

The authority of the Scriptures begins with the fact that the Godhead, through the Holy Spirit, inspired the authors and guided the community that received God's Word. God is the author of and the authority within the Holy Scriptures. The Scriptures are fully an expression of the reality of God. However, the Scriptures themselves do not surpass the authority and power of the Triune God. The Scriptures are a derivative or consequent dimension of God as God seeks to communicate through self-revelation to creation. The Scriptures as an abiding presence of God are supreme in their communications value but they do not surpass Deity itself. The Scriptures authentically flow from God. They are an extension of God—God's Word. But they are not more than personal revelation.

What is meant by affirming that "God through His Spirit inspired the authors"? The verb *inspire* comes from the Greek *theopneustos.* It means "God-spirited" or "God-breathed-out." The image of inspiration suggests that God breathed out through the mediation of the Holy Spirit and "spirited" or "inspired" the authors. This event occurred in much the same way that God, during creation, breathed into man and woman the breath of life. This same breathing out and breathing in are involved in the oral, written, and embodied living Word of the living God.

In an imaginative way, one might think of the inspiration of the biblical authors as mouth-to-mouth "inspiration." God breathed out wisdom, and the human authors inhaled or breathed it in. God's truth impregnated them; it moved into the will, desire, breath, and life of the authors. The Word of the living God, as originally expressed and experienced in the lives of the human authors, was a supremely sacred creation event itself. As least for the moments of inspiration the intimacy between God and author was the mutual breathing "out" and "in" that made them one. At the same time, of course, one affirms the distinct identities of God and the authors.

This doctrinal truth affirms that God breathed out the living Word. Thus the Scriptures are derived from God's breathing out; they did not originate in human impulse. The authority and power of the Scriptures are derived from the total process of God's initiation: His spirited, breathing-out of the Word; the authors' spirited, breathing-in of God's Word; and, the "bodying forth" of that Word. Scripture is not breathed out by human inspiration or impulse (Gal. 1:11–12; 2 Peter 1:20–21). It is not from humanity but from God.

Outsiders to that initial relational process find the image or word that best expresses that close, intimate relationship as "inspiration." To affirm the inspiration of the Scriptures assures one that God's will and intention are not lost, distorted, or deviated from in the spoken and written Word when it is embodied in the community of the faithful.

The process of inspiration cannot be accurately described as "mechanical verbal dictation," similar to the use of a dictating machine. The relationship in inspiration must not be understood as a mechanistic and deterministic connection. Inspiration is a profound, dynamic, and awesome process. It can only be misunderstood if it is seen as a mechanical "event."

The experiential limitations of the authors simply could not respond to a direct, divine mechanical injection. God's deep breaths invoke a response by the human recipient. Neither God's identity nor the authors' were altered to accommodate inspiration. God breathed out divine will, intention, and purpose, which were then accurately, faithfully, and appropriately expressed as the words of the living God. The authors breathed in; they spoke, wrote, and lived out God's Word. The Scriptures were written as a composite effort, a dual authorship. God, through the Holy Spirit is the primary author; the biblical writer who actively received and expressed that Word in human language is the secondary author. Both are equally necessary and present in the inspired writing of the Bible.

PERCEPTION AND EXPRESSION

God's revelation and inspiration are closely related in the product, the Bible. God took the initiative to inspire, to instill, to help create the theological vision in the lives of the writers. This action was effective in assuring that the initial sense perception or breathing in by the human author caught the truth and intentionality of God's will. The perceiving and recording of God's self-revelation are not a single event. They are separate stages of a sequence or a complex event that the church titles the inspiration of Scripture. God fully intended that divine truth would be expressed and recorded with complete accuracy. The inspired authoring or embodying of God's breathing out in the Scriptures is twofold: (1) It includes the authors' accurate sense *perception* of God's truth. (2) It includes the authors' accurate linguistical *expression* of God's truth.

. . . causing them to perceive God's truth and record it with accuracy.

In this study the root word *accurate* or *accuracy* was selected as the best one for expressing the full process of the inspiration of Scripture. Other commentators or theologians prefer words or phrases such as *entirely trustworthy, completely reliable, infallible, inerrant, truthful.*

In recent years the evangelical community has been engaged in a significant debate about the best words or phrases to express the orthodox, historic doctrine of the inspiration of Scripture.[10] My concern is to make a positive contribution to an evangelical understanding of the power of God in the Bible and the authority God's Word has for our lives. For a number of reasons I believe use of the word *accurate* or *accuracy* adds to a fuller understanding of the dynamics and power of the inspiration of Scripture. What is more, I believe this understanding flows out of a Wesleyan perspective and adds a

107

freshness of spirit and insight not available from other evangelical traditions.

The Wesleyan theological perspective, with its stress on holiness—in thought, word, and deed—has always been highly experiential. Stress is on the believer's personal experience of salvation and of a daily, intimate walk with Jesus that is both compassionate and disciplined. Wesleyan theology stresses the experiential in faith, and therefore a doctrine of inspiration will underscore the dynamic and relational elements of God and humanity in inspiration; in fact, inspiration itself is a dynamic process. Imagery and language may be somewhat or very similar to the expressions used by evangelicals in other faith traditions, but there is a stress on the transactional, personal process of inspiration that is distinctive in Wesleyan theology. Therefore, my preference for the word *accuracy* conveys a subtle but different sense of the experience of the authority of Scripture than appears to be the case or need in other traditions.

In this chapter the key word used to communicate the power and authority of biblical inspiration is *accuracy*. Several essential dynamic and relational issues must be considered, from a Wesleyan perspective, when the authority of the Bible is under discussion. These include the five following: (1) dual authorship—divine and human; (2) criterion for truth—faith/practice and scientific exactitude; (3) clarity and obscurity in the Scriptures; (4) concepts in Scripture—biblical vocabulary and cultural vocabulary; and (5) dual witness to God's revelation—Scripture and Spirit.

In the five issues sketched above, one is confronted by several sets of polarities that may appear to the reader as unrelated and therefore mutually exclusive. What makes the pairing of these polarities *real* issues for the evangelical is precisely their unavoidable relationship; they cannot be dismissed but neither do they yield to easy theological resolution. The task in this discussion is to resolve *how* the Wesleyan evangelical understands the dynamic relationship of these five sets of polarities that directly affect one's doctrine of inspiration.

In the preceding major division a case was presented for understanding the inspiration of the authorship of the Bible as a dual authorship. Our attention now turns to the second major polarity, the criterion of biblical truth: the truth of faith verses the truth of scientific exactitude. My view is that both are organically related and therefore cannot finally be separated except for purposes of a discussion that points up the degree of difference in emphasis.

THE PRINCIPLE OF LIMITATION IN *SOLA SCRIPTURA*

Of chief importance in scriptural authority is the Scripture's consistency and wholeness as a guide not only for saving faith but also for the daily perfecting of holiness. This is the primary theological value of the authority of Scripture. A secondary—but not unimportant—aspect of the authority of Scripture is its essential technical reliability about relationships that are perceived from a perspective that shifts from a strictly theological orientation to a scientific one. In short, the Bible is fully reliable, trustworthy, and infallible in those areas of life that are intended by God to occupy its chief concern. These areas pertain to faith and Christian discipleship and *not* to scientific specifications whose parameters are susceptible to highly variant cultural formulations.

The Enlightenment years followed close on the heels of the Protestant Reformation and the Renaissance period and brought an end to the ideological and political monopoly of the so-called Holy Roman Empire. This shift meant that many areas of thought traditionally claimed by the church and the church's theologians as its area of authority could no longer be "blessed" and safeguarded by theology, the "queen of the sciences."

This shift, commonly understood as a secularization process, means that theological leaders could no longer be expected to speak with equal vigor, integrity, and authority to *all* the adventures of the human spirit. The lurking danger of secularism is that gradually theology may find that it is unable to speak convincingly to any issue because in a secular culture theology itself is not seen as providing insightful information.

This theological predicament was in part a failure of theological nerve on the part of liberals and evangelicals alike. And it led directly into a "theology of failure": the church, its ministry, and its theology seemed to be inferior or out of touch when compared to the standards of a modern, secular world, and this failure has been praised as the church's most authentic witness.

Thomas Oden, in his important work *Agenda for Theology* suggests where this failure of theological integrity leads. For some it moves toward a total secularization. For others, including Oden himself, who spent years in disheartening chases after the secular–theme bandwagons, there comes a sudden theological judgment from God: "the central theme of contemporary theology is accommodation to modernity."[11] To counter this initially cheerful acquiescence to the intellectual climate born of Enlightenment (emphasis on human skills and initiative) parents, Oden pleads for theology to return "full circle," from classical orthodoxy to secular modernity to a "post-modern orthodoxy." His is not a call to literally duplicate the New Testament church and its cultural mores, but his "agenda" calls for the church and the theologians of the church to move beyond the seduction into modernity and recover the authority of both the Scriptures and the teaching and care of classical orthodoxy without trying to duplicate all the particulars of behavior.[12]

Holding in abeyance for the moment this pilgrimage of modern, secular, liberal theology and its future, we need to trace the pathway of evangelical orthodoxy during the same period. The key doctrines of the Protestant Reformation were *sola fide* (one is saved by "faith alone") and *sola Scriptura* (the sole, supreme authority for Christian faith and practice is the Bible and not the church). The Protestant Reformation quickly spread its two theological wings, *sola fide* and *sola Scriptura*, and moved into the Renaissance period in which the scientific method emerged as a captivating vision of reality. The scientific world view coupled with the Enlightenment's stress on rationalism were cultural allurements that put tremendous pressure on Protestant orthodoxy, especially its principle of *sola Scriptura*. The mood of the scientific and industrial revolution were woven into the theological great awakenings associated with John Wesley and Jonathan Edwards.

The liberal wing of the church moved toward secularism in response to the scientific revolution of the Enlightenment while the evangelical wing moved toward fundamentalism. Both moved for essentially the same reason: a concerted theological response to the power of rationalism in the eighteenth and nineteenth centuries. The liberals allowed both the content and the method of their theology to be dictated by the content and method of secular scientism, the end result being the emergence of a secular scholasticism. Evangelicals, too, allowed the method of their theology to be controlled by secular scientism. They held tenaciously to *sola Scriptura*. But in their preoccupation to retain the pure orthodoxy of the biblical *content*—Scripture alone is the authority for matters of salvation—they overstepped that essential principle of classical, orthodox Christianity. Persuaded by the spirit of the age out of a responsiveness to God's Holy Spirit, they gradually came to believe that theological orthodoxy required an extension of *sola Scriptura* to include both content and method of modern science. The first problem was an overextension of the fundamental theological principle, *sola Scriptura*, of the Reformation and classical Christianity. The second aspect of the problem was encouraged, not by theological insight but by the allurements of the constructs of scientific method itself. The principle of *sola Scriptura* was not, in its *formal* theological character, intended to extend to speak with equal clarity and forcefulness about the

111

material realities of theological and scientific world views. The basis for this overextension of theological truth and categories is found to reside in the intellectual spirit of the age of Enlightenment, not in any special revelation from God. Thus for the wrong theological reasons, Protestant, evangelical orthodoxy found its theological *method* controlled by precisely that secular influence that it had hoped to bring under its spiritual influence. Content and method became so inseparably related that when the intellectual control of orthodoxy's methodology slipped into the hands of scientific rationalism, the theological content itself also shifted and was altered. This change began with the welcomed inclusion of scientific methodology but quickly transformed the theological vision of the evangelicals into a defensive, historical positivism. This transformation ran quite contrary to the enlivening spirit of the orthodoxy of the Reformers Calvin and Luther and the scriptural Christianity of the Anglican Renewalist, Wesley.

Oden, in his study of modern theology, has astutely observed that the five theological fundamentals adopted as orthodoxy at the Niagara Bible Conference of 1895 are based on the premise of the *methodological* primacy of historicism. Basically fundamentalism is a theology whose conceptual categories were claimed to be found in objective historical evidence or *fact* though they omit the *experience* of prevenient grace, conviction, and repentance; the joyous triumph of being saved by grace and living in the perfecting of holiness in daily life is sadly and significantly missing.[13]

Thus the lively orthodoxy of classical Christianity became the brittle and confused scholasticism of modern theological fundamentalism. The corrective need is certainly neither an abandonment of the principle of *sola Scriptura* nor an abandonment of plenary inspiration. Rather, the task of theology is to reorient both the content and the method of orthodoxy toward its true theological area of responsibility: to record the events and share the meanings of God's redemptive activity in history that would draw men to salvation.[14] The task and responsibility is not to generalize the orthodox meaning of the supreme authority of Scripture or to catalog in exhaustive exactness the *facts* of science that do not bear directly on the message of salvation.[15] The proper scope for the authority of Scripture pertains to the matters of faith essential for salvation. The principle of *sola Scriptura* is not a treatise advocating or denying the philosophical positivism of the early-modern period of scientific empiricism. Its criterion for truth is not the coherence of the empirical "facts" of experimental physics or the data-processing predicability of computer architecture. Rather its criteria for truth are clarity and trustworthiness for salvation by faith alone.[16]

Therefore in reaffirming the principle of *sola Scriptura* in this commentary on the essentials of Wesleyan theology, care has been exercised to select words and use images that help to bring together again the content and method of evangelical orthodoxy. This allows theology to be theology and historical empiricism to be the lively methodology for a different set of principles employed within disciplines properly governed by scientific exactitude. The principle of *sola Scriptura*, however, arises out of the experience of salvation through grace by faith, not through the conceptualities distinctive to historical and scientific empiricism.

FAITH/PRACTICE AND SCIENTIFIC EXACTITUDE

The language generally associated with efforts to state the authority of Scripture stems principally from two root words, *inerrant* and *infallible*. Our understanding is formed in two ways: first, there is the etymological or technical definition and, second, there is the practical or common usage definition.

Initially we consider the strict grammatical definition of these key words. The word *inerrant* has its rootage in the Latin *inerrans*. And this word has two basic parts. First is the prefix *in*. Second is the word *errant* from *errans*, the past participle of *errare*, "to err." The English *inerrant* means "exempt from error, not errant."

The word *infallible* comes from the Latin word *infallibilis*. This word, like inerrant, is a compound word. It combines *in* and *fallible. Infallibilis* is the quality or state of being infallible, not fallible, incapable of error, unerring. These are the words used by many evangelicals to affirm the total trustworthiness of Scripture.

In preparing the *Junaluska Affirmation,* preference was expressed for the word *accurate* to express the authority and integrity of Scripture. A note about the etymology of that word would be helpful before we proceed further. The word *accurate* comes from the Latin *accuratus:* it means "prepared with care." *Accuratus* is the past participle of the Latin verb *accurare;* it means "to take care of, to do carefully." Accuracy is the state or degree of being accurate. It conforms to truth or some standard or model. It has a measured degree of conformity to some recognized standard value.

The words *infallible, inerrant,* and *accurate* are similar in their etymological rootage. However, the claim being offered here is that a real definitional difference exists. Moreover, the Wesleyan emphasis on experience carries a significant practical or operational difference that is illuminating to explore and is helpful in its pastoral effect.

Initially, a comparison of the etymological differences of the three words—inerrant, infallible, accurate—is needed. All three point to a compliance to an external standard, plan, or design. All three clearly suggest an internal consistency of that which is received—that it is essentially harmonious with the originating impulse. That is, what has been communicated has been received essentially intact. There is, however, a subtle definitional difference: infallible and inerrant are oriented along a negative axis; accurate moves along a positive axis. Infallible means "incapable of error" and inerrant means "exempt from error," whereas accurate implies a positive perspective and means "prepared with care."

The first two of the three words tend to suggest that whatever it is that is defined as infallible or inerrant, it is like a box or a rock or the recording chart of a measuring instrument. They imply a finished product, a discrete, clearly bounded object free from constructional flaws in any regard. The emphasis is on a finished, objective substance that focuses on the product itself as correct, precise, exact—a perfect product.

The word *accuracy* points less exclusively to the finished, objective product and suggests that the preparation, production, and final product was done with care, skill, and grace. It is as though a skilled artisan is offering a crafted product— exact, precise, a masterpiece to be sure, but one that has been handled by the human spirit. It thereby gains at least a measure of its value because it was crafted by human hands and not simply monitored in its automated construction by a production-line employee trained to watch dials but not to touch. *Accuracy* suggests that a product is being offered, conveyed, shared. It suggests a close personal relationship between the individual and the fruits of his labor, and that close bonding of the craftsman and his craft always makes what is offered to the public more than a finished, production-line product.

The above discussion is intended to suggest some definitional and connotative reasons for preferring *accuracy* in affirming the inspiration of Scripture. But the careful etymological distinctions are only half the story; theologically the other half of the rationale is the actual usage of the terminology and what that bears witness to theologically.

The positive axis of *accuracy* conveys the pastoral and caring component in the writing of Scripture alongside the component of precision. Truth is preserved, the design of God's revelation is followed, the Scriptures are faithful and trustworthy in what is their essential communication: God is without equal; God is Creator, Redeemer, and Sustainer of the world and all that is in it. The small prefix *in-* introduces into the actual usage of *inerrant* and *infallible* a defensive posture. When pressed, this negative axis of *in-* or *non-* locates the actual locus of importance of God's written Word, not on the relationship between God and creation—including the biblical authors—but on an objective product, as though the Bible has a life of its own independent from its being a means of expression of its divine and human authors. The Bible does not have a detached, independent life of its own. When inerrantists are crowded for a strict definition of terms, their defensive etymological distinctions in support of their position become impaled on linguistical positivism that is separated from the pastoral and relational intent of Scripture and lead more to word games than to effective proclamation and pastoral care.[17]

The power of God that causes the biblical writers "to perceive God's truth and record it with accuracy," which is what is affirmed here, is a power that binds writer and product in a way that is highly personal, historical, and relational. God's power is not arbitrary in inspiration but coordinates the achievement. The inspiration and writing of Scripture is analogous to or an exemplification of the dynamics of the faith experience. From a Wesleyan perspective, one does not think in terms of having an inerrant faith experience; it is what it is. It is recalled and lived out with the firm intent to live into holiness, to grow into perfection—a wholeness, a completeness of fellowship with the Godhead. The believer wants to live out the intensity and purpose of the close, personal saving relationship with Jesus Christ with extreme accuracy. But in the Wesleyan tradition one does not describe that relationship as inerrant or infallible; rather, it is what it is. Experience *is;* it happens; it occurs; but experience is not seen as inerrant or errant. It is the daily *struggle* to embody or show forth the spiritual power of God in one's life. But the guiding theological vision for that pilgrimage toward perfection is a journey toward accurately embodying the kingdom of God.

Holiness, or Christian perfection, cannot be detached from personal experience nor can writing the Bible be separated from the personal experience of the authors as human beings. Writing is more like an artisan activity, including the

116

idiosyncracies of the authors' cultural and psychological character, than it is a production-line activity. The unfortunate connotations of *inerrant* suggest a philosophical commitment to scientific empiricism that locates its highest value on so-called scientific exactitude rather than a faith relationship. Yet, when it comes to objective data, the original originals of the Bible are not available to us; thus, to affirm the objective truth of and connectives to the original autographs is a matter—hardly of scientific exactitude—of faith, risk, and trust. The philosophical posture advanced by an inerrantist approach functions as though it requires scientific exactitude if it is to be persuasive.[18] Scientific exactitude is not required either logically or experientially; and that is one basic reason for my preference for *accuracy.* But that preference, indeed insistence, is not solely a philosophical position; it is principally a theological orientation that flows from the life and work of John Wesley.

Perhaps John Wesley's most important theological contribution is his doctrine of sanctification, of holiness in life. The Christian moves toward a perfection that locates its completion in God. Categories of growth, change, and the maturing process in Christian faith require a notion of perfection and perfectibility not found in the rationalism of post-Reformation historical empiricism.[19]

The believer grows in grace and moves toward perfection; and there is a responsiveness experienced by the believer and God. Growth in Christian experience is actual and real. It is made possible and received by God the author and perfecter of our faith. God really responds to a believer's growing maturity in Christ. But transcending God's responsiveness is God's immutable character, and it remains unaffected by a Christian's growth in grace. Because believers are in Christ, they have full fellowship with the Godhead.[20]

Perfection, experientially, is a matter of growth, change, and maturity in the Christian life. Perfection is to be understood in categories and dimensions that transcend the "pure" immutability, unchangeableness, and unresponsiveness of medieval scholasticism.

In short, perfection in faith surpasses immutability. The perfecting of holiness includes potential for responsiveness and change. Responsiveness and an unchanging identity coexist in the Christian's life in Christ.

The two major biblical and doctrinal realities of "scriptural Christianity" *(experience* and *growth* in grace) transcend a theology that is oriented toward imposing twentieth-century standards for exactitude of measurement on matters of inspiration of Scripture, which ultimately is a matter of faith both originally and now.

The Scottish church historian Thomas Lindsay argued at the turn of the century for the concern presented here. He said, as quoted by Rogers and McKim:

> Infallibility does not consist in formal inerrancy at all, but in the power which compels me to know that God is through the Scripture speaking to me now as He spoke not merely *by* the prophets and holy men of old, but *to* them and *in* them, and giving me through them in Word and picture the message of His salvation. . . .
>
> The Reformers did not take Inspiration to mean a Divine superintendence exercised over the writers of Scripture in order to produce an errorless record.[21]

Lindsay's own preference was for an understanding of the inspiration of Scripture far closer to the position advocated here. Stress, for him, was placed on a "coordination of achievement" in which words like *conveys, offers,* and *records* are seen to fully represent the inspired transaction. Stress is given to function and organic unity. There is an affirmation of mutual responsiveness, freedom, coordination, indeed of "achievement."[22]

Finally, the theological principle, *sola Scriptura*, is a relational concept as much as it is a product description. In fact, *sola Scriptura* is an operational principle. The authority of Scripture does not exist apart from its actual usage. If the

Scriptures were not put to actual use, their authority would be like the sound of a tree falling in a forest where no one is present to hear: there would be no sound; there would be no authority. The Scriptures gain their power in their usage, in the actuality of facilitating both a saving relationship with God and a daily, disciplined walk with the Lord Jesus Christ.

The mechanistic and deterministic premises of scientific positivism associated with the words *infallible* and *inerrant* compel one to seek a more helpful synonym. Therefore the word *accurate* was selected. There is no diminution of intention or clarity in the preference for *accurate*. To do something with accuracy means that the product is correct, exact, and precise. Accuracy is the state or degree of being accurate: whatever is accurate conforms to truth or some standard or model, a measured degree of conformity to some recognized standard value.

THE "ORIGINAL AUTOGRAPHS" AND THE WITNESS OF THE SPIRIT

The objectification of Scripture—its writing—is the final cause of the inspiration of Scripture. The Scriptures offer a new cause for hope for any reader. The accuracy of the Holy Scriptures extends beyond the initial objective statement of God's Word, the "original autographs of the Holy Scripture."

The initial receiving or inspiring of God's Word is not a priori exempt from the possiblity of error; that is, the Scriptures are not a box of truth deposited on the human scene without human interaction. And that interaction is true of the formation of the original autographs and of any subsequent reading, hearing, or beholding of God's Word.

The original autographs of Holy Scripture and their interpretation could, perhaps, be guaranteed errorless by logical argumentation. But the original and subsequent hearing, writing, and speaking cannot be guaranteed before their occurrence to be errorless, completely accurate, having no novelty whatsoever. Individuality, creativity, and autonomy exert themselves. As one reads God's Word, it has the power to change that person. There is an interaction between the reader and the Word. Reading the Scriptures offers the possibility for conformity between the reader's understanding and God's objective intention, but this is not guaranteed in advance.

The evangelical recognizes this truth and openly stresses prayerful, careful, deliberate, reverent, and disciplined reading of the Scriptures. The efficacy, authority, and effect of the Scriptures upon the reader, hearer, beholder, or writer depends in measure on the personal attitude, purpose, and aim taken in regard to the Scriptures and one's openness to the leading of the Holy Spirit. On a purely human plane, misinterpretation and distortion of the Word of God is not only possible but entirely likely.

PLENARY INSPIRATION OF SCRIPTURE
AND CULTURAL VOCABULARY

The inspiration of the Scriptures includes plenary inspiration. The word *plenary* means "full." It refers to whether or not all Scripture is "equally" inspired. The inspiration of the Scriptures is the expression of God's Word with *accuracy;* thus the *full* inspiration of the Scriptures is affirmed. One notes that in the Protestant tradition, expecially in the theology of Martin Luther, there has been the idea of "a canon within a canon." This teaching refers to those special areas of the Scriptures that are more edifying for salvation than other portions. This, too, is affirmed.

Modern, liberal theologians depart from Luther, Protestant orthodoxy, and the church fathers and anchor their conceptualities in a cultural vocabulary, not in the biblical vocabulary. They claim that biblical writings only *contain* the Word of God, like a bucket half-filled with water. They make a distinction between scriptural passages that are considered essential for salvation and other passages that, they maintain, certainly are not inspired. This attitude represents a sharp departure from the views of Luther, Calvin, and Wesley. The partially-full-container view of inspired Scripture results from a fractured or broken doctrine of inspiration; it is not plenary inspiration that is affirmed. By contrast, the Wesleyan position affirms that God, in wholeness, relates and reveals the Word to us in the full range of human experience.

ABIDING INSPIRATION HOLDS TOGETHER THE CLARITY
AND OBSCURITY OF SCRIPTURE

Previous discussion in this chapter has focused on the inspiration of the original autographs. Attention now turns from original autographs to the present. The initial inspiration refers to the recording of God's truth. It is the inspiring of the initial revelation: the eternal presence of God's Holy Spirit in the intellectual processes of the authors and in the activity of recording God's truth. That sequence is complex and involves inspiration at each stage.[23]

It is evident that the Holy Scriptures have been preserved during the long process of transmission through copyists and translators, and we attribute such accurate preservation to the work of the Holy Spirit.

The Scriptures were inspired at their inception and in their transmission, preservation, and lively witness. The Scriptures accurately express God's truth in the original revelatory event. Scriptural Christianity also affirms that the Holy Scriptures have been preserved accurately in the long process of transmission, in the life of the Israelites, in the life of the Christian church, and in the lives of believers.[24] This preservation, like the initial inspiration, is interactional. The Holy Spirit interacts with persons, cultures, congregations, and communities where the Scriptures are read and heard to illuminate that reading and hearing of God's holy Word. But this illumination of one's intellect and spiritual nerve centers is not mechanical; it is not a function purely of the "head" or intellect. Illumination and guidance occur in the "heart" as well as the "head."

121

Believers are assured of the continual efficacy of the Scriptures in varied contemporary expressions: language, imagery, translation, paraphrases, and various types of rendition. The Holy Spirit works through the various translations and paraphrases to preserve the essential truths of God's revelation. The Holy Spirit stands at the center of the life of the Christian community, guiding believers toward sufficient clarity in discerning God's truth for the contemporary follower.

THE AUTHORITY OF THE SCRIPTURES

At the beginning of this chapter, the Scriptures were affirmed as transcending the teaching and authority of the church. Alongside that is the emphasis on the contemporary believer's need for a reverent and disciplined study of the Scripture, all to be guided and illuminated by the Holy Spirit.

These Scriptures are supremely authoritative for the Church's teaching, preaching, witness, identifying error, correcting the erring, and training believers for ministry in and through the Church.

The scope and strength of the Holy Spirit's work in illumination is illustrated by the following excerpt from The Junaluska Affirmation statement on the Holy Spirit:

> He bears witness to Christ and guides God's people into His truth. He inspired the Holy Scripture, God's written Word, and continues to illuminate His people concerning His will and truth. His guidance is always in harmony with Christ and the truth as given in the Holy Scriptures.

It is imperative to affirm the responsibility of the church to use the Scriptures fully in all its activities; the Scriptures are authoritative for *all* activities of the ministry and mission of the church. "All Scripture is God-breathed and is useful for teaching, rebuking, correcting, and for training in righteousness, that the [men and women] of God may be thoroughly equipped for every good work" (2 Tim. 3:16–17).

Receiving the Scriptures as the inspired Word of God is

essential. Equally important is to understand how the Bible is interpreted or put to work. This is the area of methodology or hermeneutics. Brief guidelines for biblical hermeneutics are these: (1) A passage of Scripture should be accepted in its customary, socially acknowledged literal meaning unless the context dictates otherwise. (2) Critical extrabiblical efforts to discern the truths of the particulars of a text should be subordinated, ultimately, to the text; the Bible can best answer questions about itself.[25] (3) From church history, St. Augustine offers this:

> If you chance upon anything in Scripture that does not seem to be true, you must not conclude that the sacred writer made a mistake; rather your attitude should be: the manuscript is faulty, or the version is not accurate, or you yourself do not understand the matter.[26]

The Scriptures are included in the church's teaching ministry. Truly what the church receives as doctrine and teaching is the fountainhead of its interpretive activities: "preaching, witnessing, identifying error, correcting the erring, and training believers for ministry in and through the Church."

The Scriptures are central for the life of the congregation *within* the church, and *through* the church as a public, corporate institution and social force of mission and ministry in the community and world at large.

DISCUSSION QUESTIONS

1. Do you believe that the Scriptures contain all that is necessary for us to learn of our need for salvation, to respond and grow in the faith?

2. What is the importance of the doctrine *sola Scriptura*?

3. What is your view of the inspiration of Scripture and how does that relate to the claim for infallibility or inerrancy of Scripture? What is at stake in this theological debate?

4. Why does the scriptural Christianity position affirm the "continuing inspiration" of Scripture through the Holy Spirit?

5. What is the proper role of Scripture in the ministries of the local church?

SALVATION

Scriptural Christianity affirms that God offers salvation to a sinful humanity and a lost world through Jesus Christ. By His death on the cross the sinless Son propitiated the holy wrath of the Father, a righteous anger occasioned by sin. By His resurrection from the dead, the glorified Son raises us to newness of life. When we appropriate by faith God's atoning work in Jesus Christ we are forgiven, justified, regenerated by His Holy Spirit, and adopted into the family of God. By His grace He sanctifies His children, purifying their hearts by faith, renewing them in the image of God, and enabling them to love God and neighbor with whole heart. The fullness of God's great salvation will come with the return of Christ. This cosmic event will signal the resurrection of the saved to eternal life and the lost to eternal damnation, the liberation of creation from the Adamic curse, God's final victory over every power and dominion, and the establishment of the new heaven and the new earth.

THE OFFER OF SALVATION

God is the author of salvation. We cannot save ourselves. We are not the authors of our own salvation. Salvation begins in God's initiative. Salvation is God's act of grace toward sinners. It does not begin in the sinner's heart. Wesley said, "No man loves God by nature, any more than he does a stone, or the earth he treads upon."[1]

Scriptural Christianity affirms that God offers salvation to a sinful humanity and a lost world through Jesus Christ.

God first offers salvation to a sinful humanity, the crowning act of creation. But we are not saved in separation from, nor taken out of, a lost world. Salvation is extended to the entire lost world. All creation is bound together in the need for salvation.

In God's offer of salvation to all creation resides the hope for a new creation in Christ. The world will be reconciled and made new in Christ Jesus. Through God the Son reconciliation is achieved with the fullness of the Godhead—God the Father, Son, and Holy Spirit.

Salvation is offered through a specific means, Jesus Christ. It is achieved through the person and work of Jesus of Nazareth, the Christ. This chapter therefore concentrates on the means by which grace is appropriated to salvation.

THE SPECIFIC MEANS OF GRACE

By His death on the cross the sinless Son propitiated the holy wrath of the Father, a righteous anger occasioned by sin.

There are three important facets to God's saving grace that are affirmed in Wesleyan theology.

First, God's grace is made available through the incarnation of His Son who lived and died that sinners might receive God's grace and the new birth. Jesus suffered and died on a cross. His death was an objective, historical reality. The crucifixion occurred at a specific point in time and in a specific geographical location.

126

Christian tradition affirms this saving action as the finality of Jesus Christ. This means that Jesus, through His death, made an offering of Himself. The direct and final result of this action is that salvation is possible for all who believe. Without Christ's death, God's offer of salvation would have been little more than a vain hope for both God and humanity.

Beginning with creation, God endeavored to establish the circumstance in which creation would enjoy a full and harmonious relationship with God. With the fall of Adam and Eve that initial fellowship was broken and thereby the original righteous, or perfect, fellowship was lost. On numerous occasions God took the initiative to reestablish that original relationship through His grace. Among the most notable examples are the deliverance of Israel from Egyptian bondage (Exod. 12–15) and the giving of the Ten Commandments (Exod. 20; Deut. 5). The fact that sin kept breaking the relationship and God kept offering opportunities for Israel to enter into reconciliation with God is the salvation history that is the story of both Old and New Testaments. Contemporary biblical theologians call this *Heilsgeschichte,* a German word meaning "salvation history." Indeed, the tracing of God's relationship with Israel and all of humanity is a history of God's repeated efforts in offering divine grace to bring about salvation. But we all resist. The finality aspect of Jesus Christ is that Jesus, the Son, is the final, supreme, ultimate effort by God to offer salvation. Beyond God's only Son Jesus Christ God has no other means by which to offer salvation. In affirming the finality of Jesus Christ, one acknowledges that nothing beyond Jesus Christ is necessary for salvation and beyond Jesus Christ God has no other means of grace available by which we may be saved.

Second, God's grace occurs only within specific, historical activities or events. Salvation is possible only through the sacrificial death of Jesus. The highest and final effort by God in offering salvation was in the Son, Jesus. The highest and ultimate offering by humans to any god is a human sacrifice.

The very idea that Christianity is based on the sacrificial death of a human being seems offensive, primordial, even evil. Revulsion toward the religious sacrifice of another is perhaps universal. But nonetheless Jesus was sacrificed on the cross. That is why we understand Jesus' death as the scandal of the cross.

But Jesus' death on the cross is not solely a human effort to please or appease God. In Jesus, second person of the Trinity, God too is present and therefore suffers and is crucified ever as much as the human dimension of Jesus. In Jesus' sacrificial death God both gives a sacrifice and receives a sacrifice, suffers and is satisfied, and thereby redeems. In Jesus' death the sacrifice of God and man is most fully and finally joined. Beyond that, God and humanity simply cannot go.

Thus we cannot depreciate the historical, sacrificial nature of Jesus' death on the cross by trying to be "nice" and go "easy" on the sacrificial means of grace. We are involved in the scandal of the cross. To turn aside the supreme and final effort by God to offer salvation in the death and resurrection of Jesus Christ is to flee from salvation itself. We dare not undercut God's crucifixion in Jesus Christ in a vain struggle to make more pleasing and less primitive both the nature and depth of human sin and the nature and depths of God's grace to save us.

Jesus' death is not a spiritual vapor, nor a poetic expression, nor a theological metaphor for a bland, mutual acceptance of God and humanity. Salvation is made possible for us through the historical suffering, death, and resurrection of Jesus Christ.

Third, the Son's death produces saving consequences. The "sinless Son"—to borrow a phrase from John Calvin—has set aside, or appeased, God's holy wrath and righteous anger because of human sin.

The doctrine of propitiation (appeasement) of God may be unacceptable to some who prefer to avoid a theological affirmation of God's wrath and anger. To avert one's face from

128

this scriptural truth is to hide in the enormity and pervasiveness of sin and to refuse to face the theological reality of sin. The words *wrath* or *anger* are theological terms, not principally psychological. We ought not to confuse psychological sensitivities with theological truths.

God's wrath is a holy and righteous anger. It is brought about by our willful violation of God's purpose in creation, not by a distempered spirit in God. Christ did not come nor die to appease the ill temper of a tribal, vindictive god. The wrath and anger affirmed in Scriptures are not the raw emotions of a primitive, bestial god (Gen. 6:6; Exod. 20:5; Lev. 20:23; Deut. 29:20). Our sinful vanity causes us to mislocate the theological truth of God's wrath and anger. But God's righteous anger is not evoked by any emotional instability in Him. It is aroused by the disobedience of a fallen and falling world.[2]

Traditional Wesleyan theology affirms that the person of God has been offended and violated, not by sociological snubs, but by sin—the human predisposition to replace God with ourselves as the ruler of the universe. Outward and inward violations and offenses exist. God's righteous anger and holy wrath are proper responses to what we have done. The sinful humanity and lost world that we are is what provokes God's inherent gracious and loving nature and challenges His wisdom and leadership in creation. The temptation in Genesis 2–3 has its focus in our human passion to know absolutely everything and to be leader of all. God said, "But you must not eat from the tree of the knowledge of good and evil, for when you eat of it you will surely die" (Gen. 2:17). It is we who provoke God by endeavoring to claim perfect wisdom and knowledge for ourselves.

Humanity was created to enjoy God, the Holy One, forever. To experience a holy relationship evokes awe, mystery, and an awareness of the transcendence of God. Sin is a response that violates our holy respect for God's transcendence and immanence, a presence both distant and near that we cannot attain or encompass. Sin is our substitution of human achievement and pride for holy awe of the Triune God. Human pride breaks the relationship that God intends and it kindles His anger. Basic aspects of God's person and purpose both in what has been created and in what God desires are violated by our intentional pride.

Our refusal to accept our limits, our substitution of our will for God's, and our destruction of a trusting, holy relationship are what evoke God's holy anger. God's anger has both an inner effect (God's feelings) and an outer effect (God's action in His relation to creation).

Since God's anger was evoked when grace and love were first offered, what can now set aside the wrath stirred by human, prideful sin? Certainly nothing of purely human origin can. The one who can set aside, or appease, God's wrath is none other than the Son, Jesus Christ.

The propitiation of God's wrath and anger by Jesus' sacrificial death sets aside our condemnation that was rightfully deserved because of our sin: "Just as the result of one trespass was condemnation for all men, so also the result of one act of righteousness was justification that brings life for all men" (Rom. 5:18). "Therefore, there is now no condemnation for those who are in Christ Jesus" (8:1).

The need for grace and the provision for the specific means of salvation can be clearly demonstrated. God offers salvation, the gift of redeeming grace that removes condemnation in Jesus Christ, by His death on the cross.

A profound truth was uttered by God to Israel: "You only have I chosen of all the families of the earth; therefore I will punish you for all your sins" (Amos 3:2). Those who are chosen, whether of the house of Israel or of the Christian church, participate more fully in the holiness and righteousness of God. Those nearest the center of the power and likeness of God are those who will also receive punishment for all their sins. "From everyone who has been given much, much will be demanded" (Luke 12:48). God's punishment is not capricious or vindictive. It does not fall on the unsuspecting or naive. Rather, it is an anger for those who know the purpose of God and scorn repentance.

In Gethsemane and on the cross, God concentrated His wrath on one Person. Any lingering pretense to protect God from human images of psychological and parental wrath and anger must be dismissed. God protected neither Himself nor His Son from wrath and anger. Jesus experienced the full weight of God's wrath, abandonment, curse, and rejection on the cross (Pss. 22:1; 60:3; Isa. 51:17; Matt. 27:46; Mark 15:34).

Jesus' death on the cross lifts the wrath of God from the sinner (Rom. 5:9; 1 Thess. 1:10). "God made him who had no sin to be sin for us, so that in him we might become the righteousness of God" (2 Cor. 5:21).

Jesus the Christ set aside the wrath and anger of God that was caused by human sin so that in Him we might be made holy and righteous before God.

SHARING IN THE RESURRECTION

Jesus' resurrection from the dead was total, body and spirit. Wesley, Calvin, and Luther alike accept what the Scriptures say about Jesus' resurrection.

By His resurrection from the dead, the glorified Son raises us to newness of life.

There is a dual character to Jesus' resurrection, and both aspects of that resurrection must be honored and taught in the church: Jesus' resurrection included both body and spirit, and each is related to the other in a transformed fashion.

The more difficult aspect of the resurrection for modern man to believe is the bodily portion. Clearly the belief and teaching of the early church as shared in the Scriptures affirms that Jesus' body was raised from death (Luke 24:3, 39–43; 1 Cor. 15; Col. 2:9). The New Testament is not overbearing about what was obvious to all. Being raised from the dead, being resurrected, carries all the common-sense qualities that the disciples, beginning with Mary Magdalene, witnessed. First-hand testimony reveals that at least one prominent post-Easter feature of Jesus' ministry was His physical presence among the disciples. This is not to argue that Jesus' body had not in fact undergone miraculous transformation. It had. But there was continuity in Jesus' life between His pre- and post-Easter body. That continuity was not just in the minds of His followers. All accounts of Scripture both directly and indirectly affirm and assume the physical reality of Jesus following Easter morning.

Two theological truths need to be set straight: (1) Jesus' post-Easter presence included a physical body, transformed in its resurrection from death. But that resurrected body was not a literal reincarnation of His precrucifixion body. It was a body transformed and possessed of a new relationship of spirit and flesh. It included physical flesh as part of its essential characteristics. (2) The resurrected presence of Jesus was more than either a body housing a sacred soul or a spiritual essence disembodied from the grave and relocated in the thoughts and memories of the believers. Jesus was not reduced to a spirit flowing from memories that began Easter morning.

Thus we maintain the dual character of the resurrected Lord: a transformed body and a spirit, fully unified and fully present to all. Jesus' ministry following Easter did not occur in a dead body reenergized like a recharged battery. Nor was it the electric current of a spiritual presence flowing freely without reference to any physical reality. The Scriptures teach and Christian orthodoxy has affirmed that both dimensions are fully present. We can affirm no less.

Beyond this kind of factual dimension of Jesus' resurrection is another important but secondary dimension. This is the meaning people attach to the resurrection. One cannot affirm Jesus' resurrection as fact apart from ascribing some meaning to that event in everyday life. The missionary stories in the book of Acts are about the theological struggles to relate fact and meaning. Some related the two beautifully (cf. Peter's Pentecost sermon, his Joppa vision of the inclusiveness of the gospel, and Paul's conversion experience and pastoral leadership). Others were unable to catch an integrated theological vision of the resurrected Lord (e.g., Ananias and Sapphira; King Agrippa).

The resurrected Son is the glorified Son. There is a preeminent newness to Jesus following the resurrection. By means of His resurrection victory and His glorification, Christ raises those who do truly and earnestly repent of their sins to a newness of life like His own.

Thus we affirm three dimensions to the resurrection: (1) the resurrected person (body and spirit) of Christ, (2) the creative transformation of the glorified Son by God the Father, and (3) the invitation to a similar resurrection for all who believe.

ADOPTION INTO GOD'S FAMILY

This statement is a declaration that affirms that the atoning work of Jesus Christ is primary in the Christian faith. Atonement occurs through (1) Jesus' death, (2) His resurrection (the effecting of the new covenant in the glorified Lord), and (3) the resultant offer of grace by God through Jesus Christ.

When we appropriate by faith God's atoning work in Jesus Christ we are forgiven, justified, regenerated by His Holy Spirit, and adopted into the family of God.

This statement is also propositional. It places salvation in real time and space. Faith is conditioned by history. Salvation is appropriated by faith in *God's atoning work* on the cross and in history.

Saving faith is a composite of four factors: (1) an awareness of sin; (2) a turning toward God through the prevenient grace of the Holy Spirit, who convicts and woos; (3) repentance and confession that sin has separated from the grace of God and kept the new covenant from being joined; and (4) personal appropriation of the new birth in Jesus Christ.

This is the basis of saving faith: forgiveness, justification, and regeneration. This threefold new life is the initial phase in becoming saved. Beyond this stage, one moves to appropriate in fullness the Spirit of Christ in daily life.

The acts of forgiveness, justification, and regeneration constitute a theological midpoint in one's life in Christ. The initial three-phase step is but half of the glorious work of salvation.

Growing in faith begins as God accepts and adopts the believer "into the family of God." The new Christian becomes a babe in Christ. The new birth is not a still birth. It is the beginning of a life that is to be nurtured, disciplined, and loved. In the ministry of the church, one begins to experience the wholeness, oneness, and unity of the family of God. Believers are brought into the household of faith and find spiritual growth and maturity in the image of Christ.

RENEWAL IN THE IMAGE OF GOD

The sinner is saved by grace through faith (Eph. 2:8), and in grace God begins the sanctification process. God's grace extends to dimensions of salvation, including sanctification. Through sanctifying grace God begins a purifying process, perfecting the believer in holiness.

By His grace He sanctifies His children, purifying their hearts by faith, renewing them in the image of God, and enabling them to love God and neighbor with whole heart.

God permeates Christian experience, unifying and moving the new children in the family of God toward full spiritual maturity.

The phrase "purifying their hearts by faith" refers to the total life, to the whole person. Purifying the heart includes a thorough cleansing of all areas of one's life. There is a re-creating, a transforming, and a bringing to life of the dormant potentiality for fellowship with God that in the unrepentant sinner is obscured by the impurities of human pride.

John Wesley's notion of practical sanctification expresses well the concern that without holiness no man shall see the Lord;—that this holiness is the work of God, who worketh in us both to will and to do;—that he doeth of his own good pleasure, merely for the merits of Christ;—that this holiness is the mind that was in Christ, enabling us to walk as he also walked;—that no man can be thus sanctified till he be justified;—and, that we are justified by faith alone.[3]

Sanctification and holiness are approximate equivalents. They indicate the nature and the goal of the life in Christ in everyday experience.

Salvation and justification are granted by God and occur in faith. The continuation of salvation through sanctification is also granted in faith. The believer is not left to wonder about the practical implications of holiness; he is renewed in the image and likeness of God. Following the new birth, what was dormant within is brought to life, prompting a rediscovery of all that God intends Christians to be in Christ.

In sanctification one moves toward the full promise inherent in being created in the image of God. One is enabled to love God and neighbor with the whole heart. To love God and neighbor with completeness and wholeness is the goal of sanctification.

One is not to love neighbor above God. They both call forth respect, love, and service. God is God, but God is never God for the believer without at the same time affirming His presence in the neighbor. One cannot separate ultimately the character of God as God from the character of neighbor as neighbor. The neighbor belongs to God and is a gift of God's presence. The believer is sanctified in relation to the neighbor.

The believer relates to God and neighbor with the whole heart, affirming the transcendent reality of God and the command to regard one's neighbor on equal footing with oneself. Both God and neighbor extend beyond the self and what can be expected of the self in isolation. God is always present in the neighbor.

135

THE CULMINATION OF SALVATION

Be patient, there is more to come! This is the promise of the ultimate relationship of believers with God in Christ. Salvation will reach God's perfect goal and be realized in the return of Christ. His purifying and enabling power will set believers free to love God and neighbor without limit or reservation, eternally.

The fullness of God's great salvation will come with the return of Christ.

THE MAKING OF ALL THINGS NEW

It may not seem pleasant to discuss the holy wrath and righteous anger of God. It is certainly less inviting to speak about eternal damnation as a theological truth. But there it is.[4] If God's holy wrath has not been reconciled and laid aside through Jesus the Son, the consequences are apparent. Men and women who continue to be unresponsive to God's grace and decide to misuse their human freedom by rejecting God and His gracious gift of salvation will invariably reap the results. God's offer of salvation has been given, and the means of salvation have been made clear in the Scriptures. If people do not appropriate God's grace through faith, the outcome is everlasting damnation. The Bible is absolutely, unequivocally clear about that.

This cosmic event will signal the resurrection of the saved to eternal life and the lost to eternal damnation, the liberation of creation from the Adamic curse, God's final victory over every power and dominion, and the establishment of the new heaven and the new earth.

There can be no rejoicing in heaven over any who are lost. But with an awesome sense of holy fear, believers will be eternally separated from the wicked. Only in the fulfillment of such promises will the words prayed so often by the church be realized: "Your will be done on earth as it is in heaven" (Matt. 6:10).

There is for all a road that forks in two directions; one path leads into God's everlasting presence, the other path leads into eternal separation from God.

Some may wonder about the absense of the words *heaven* and *hell* in this discussion. The decision not to use these terms stems from traditional theological language that locates heaven (up) and hell (down) in geophysical spots that seem too specific.

What is affirmed is a cosmic event. It is eternal. It is universal. It has specific consequences. What we affirm surely is gathered up in the traditional meaning of the terms *heaven* and *hell*. Some Christians tend to overload these theological (eschatological) truths with emotional needs. The theme of Christ's return is celebration for the believer. Herein the fullness of God's power is joyfully exhibited in the victory over evil!

Victory over evil will be complete. Creation will be liberated from the Adamic curse, from the destruction and the obscuring of original righteousness.

All powers and dominions are in principle defeated and overcome in Christ's victory (Col. 1:15–20).

A new heaven and a new earth will be firmly established. The First-born of all creation will establish a new heaven and a new earth.

DISCUSSION QUESTIONS

1. Do you have problems understanding the wrath and anger of God? Does this chapter help to clarify the problem for you? What did you learn about yourself and God?

2. Is belief in the bodily resurrection important or not? Why?

3. What is sanctification? How is it related to justification?

4. How will Christ, in His return, bring about the fullness of salvation?

5. Why is the establishment of the new heaven and new earth an occasion for joy and celebration?

THE
CHURCH

Scriptural Christianity affirms that the Church of Jesus Christ is the community of all true believers under His sovereign Lordship. This Church, the Body of Christ, is one *because it shares one Lord, one faith, one baptism. It is* holy *because it belongs to God and is set apart for His purposes in the world. It is* apostolic *because it partakes of the authority granted to the apostles by Christ Himself. It is* universal *because it includes all believers, both living and dead, in every nation, regardless of denominational affiliation. Its authenticity is to be found wherever the pure Word of God is preached and taught; wherever the Sacraments of Baptism and Holy Communion are celebrated in obedience to Christ's command; wherever the gifts of the Holy Spirit upbuild the body and bring spiritual growth; wherever the Spirit of God creates a loving, caring fellowship, and a faithfulness in witness and service to the world; and wherever discipline is administered with love under the guidance of the Word of God. The Church, as the Bride of Christ, will ultimately be joined with her Lord in triumphant glory.*

In its congregational forms the church has universal dimensions. Because of the spiritual void evident in their established churches, many Christians are encouraged to turn to camp meetings, small group Bible studies, prayer-and-share groups, charismatic cells, and so forth. The growth of so-called independent and parachurch groups has mushroomed in the past twenty years. These groups include persuasions that range from radical social activism to fundamentalism. In the face of this fragmentation, an affirmative word about the universal, corporate nature of the people of God deserves widespread hearing.

God's church universal is not dependent on the activities and understandings of people who may think that Christianity can be encompassed by isolated activities such as Bible study or social action without participating in the liturgical life of the "called community." What is needed is an embracing of the totality of the church of Jesus Christ in its particular ministries as well as in its universal, sacramental character.

THE ESSENCE OF THE CHURCH

The church universal is the dwelling place of the Triune God and is under the Godhead's lordship. The church of Jesus Christ is the intimate organic union of the church as a sociological organization. It is a spiritual communion of saints in Jesus Christ, who is the church's one foundation.

Scriptural Christianity affirms that the Church of Jesus Christ is the community of all true believers under His sovereign Lordship.

The church is a community composed of all true believers under the lordship of Jesus Christ. The church is in Christ and inseparable from Him. The visible community of all true believers is indivisible from their Lord, who is also one with the Father and the Holy Spirit. The community that does not perceive itself as under the lordship of Christ, whatever name it claims, is not the church of Jesus Christ.

Individual church leaders may be faithful, wise, and gracious, but the pastoral leadership that the clergy and priests offer in the activities of worship, adoration, and adulation is properly under the sovereign leadership of the Deity. Those groups that are unable or unwilling to acknowledge the full leadership of the Trinity in the totality of life cannot be identified as Christian.

The community of true believers includes all who profess Jesus Christ as Savior and Lord. The church is both a mystical and a sociological body. The church is of Jesus Christ and in all respects is under His sovereign lordship. Samuel J. Stone penned this affirmation in his familiar hymn, "The Church's One Foundation Is Jesus Christ Her Lord."

THE ONENESS OF THE CHURCH

There is an organic unity of believers with Christ. To affirm that the church is the body of Christ is to affirm the unity of Christ in the church. All who participate in the church participate in this unity. All are of one body despite wide divergencies in cultural background, geographical location, and personality characteristics.

This Church, the Body of Christ, is one because it shares one Lord, one faith, one baptism.

The apostle Paul uses the metaphor of the body to affirm this unity of the church and Christ (Eph. 4:4–6).

The basis of the unity in the church is the *one Lord.* God offers salvation through Jesus Christ alone. That salvation is made available to all. He provides the only way of salvation (John 5:30–47). Jesus becomes Lord in one's life when confession is made that Jesus is the Christ, the Son of God.

There is only one means by which the sinner can be saved. This is the principle of *sola fide,* by faith alone. Good works do not save. Nominal membership in a local congregation does not save. It is only through grace by faith that we are saved (Eph. 2:8). There is *one faith,* centered in Jesus Christ and resting on the witness of the Scripture to God's abiding presence.

141

The *one baptism* symbolizes being buried with, and resurrected in, Jesus Christ. "One baptism" is not a limited reference to water baptism. The Holy Spirit baptizes the believer, whatever the manner. Baptism means that one is buried and raised in Christ. The believer is in Christ. This is the one baptism.

THE HOLINESS OF THE CHURCH

The church belongs to God. Similarly, believers, reborn and being re-created in the image of God, belong to God. God, through the Son and the Holy Spirit, established the church. The church is God's. The church is the body of Christ in its organic unity and participates in the fullness of God; therefore, the church is holy.

It is holy because it belongs to God and is set apart for His purposes in the world.

The holiness that occasions the church's oneness with God does not set the church aside *from* service. Rather, it sets the church aside *for* service. The church set apart for witness will be the church triumphant. Being set apart makes the church the chosen people of God, called to exemplify its unity with the Godhead throughout the world. The entire church is called to take the whole gospel to the whole world.

The church is not "owned" by any particular faith, institution, or denomination. It is not the "possession" of any particular geographical location, national heritage, social group, economic class, political system, or human ideology. The church's life is manifested in believers who are, above all, faithful to Christ. In its social and cultural settings, the church's holy manifestations are diverse without limit, empowering evangelism, teaching, and missions.

The church expresses and echoes the purposes of God. The first purpose is to offer salvation; then, as a result of salvation, the church offers works as the loving expression of gratitude for new life received in Christ. In short, the holiness of the church is a holiness in service.

THE APOSTOLICITY OF THE CHURCH

The church partakes of the authority granted to the apostles by Christ. That authority is the rightful inheritance of all who follow after the original apostles and declare to Jesus, "My Lord and my God" (John 20:28). It is granted without reservation to those who trust in Christ. The church is one in its organic unity with God. It is holy and participates in the inner nature of God. The authority granted to the church in its apostolic function of witnessing and service is without limit.

It is apostolic because it partakes of the authority granted to the apostles by Christ Himself.

Divine authority was granted to the apostles and, through them, to all who believe. No preeminent authority has been granted exclusively to any one person, apostle, or group. Rather, authority is granted to all who follow Christ, beginning with Jesus' original apostles. Through the centuries, authority has flowed to all who have walked by faith in each new generation—to those whose relationship to God has been *sola fide* (by faith alone). The Scriptures teach that faith is the only requirement for receiving apostolic authority. In the faith relationship with Christ, authority is confirmed and granted according to those principles set forth in the Bible.

Apostolic authority continues on. Its foundation is in those who have preceded, living *sola fide*. This includes Peter as one among several original apostles. Through the witness and practice of the Holy Spirit, God continues to grant authority to the children of God to exemplify God's gracious offer of salvation and unreserved service.

THE UNIVERSALITY OF THE CHURCH

There are no organizational restrictions on those who are included in the universal church. The church includes all believers who are in clearly identifiable organizations; it also includes all who faithfully walk with God but are not in clearly

It is universal *because it includes all believers, both living and dead, in every nation, regardless of denominational affiliation.* identifiable organizations. The universal church does not include those who have never trusted Christ, regardless of their church membership or ordination. The universality of the church of Jesus Christ is not universalism. Universality means that there are no limits of time and space, organization, or visible and invisible groupings that would interfere with the nature and inclusiveness of the universal church.

This inclusiveness extends to all who have lived by faith and confessed the lordship of Jesus Christ. It began with the very first Christians, now long dead, and includes present-day Christians. The church refers to this unending fellowship as the "communion of saints."

THE AUTHENTICITY OF THE CHURCH

The phrase "the pure Word of God" affirms that God's Word proceeds from God. It does

Its authenticity is to be found wherever the pure Word of God is preached and taught . . . not originate in the hearts and lives of men and women. The living focus of the church begins with the Word of God. The word "pure" affirms the Bible's origin in the Holy Godhead, the Triune God.

This pure strand is inspired in its written form. The pure Word of God has authority as such. This purity is expressed by the twofold truths stated in chapter 7: God's truth is (1) clearly revealed in, and (2) plainly established by, God's Word, the Bible. Lay people and clergy are to study the Scriptures with a prayerful, open attitude.

From the beginning the true church of Jesus Christ has had a twofold witness to its reality: (1) it is where the Word of God is preached, and (2) it is where the Word of God is taught. The Word of God is necessary for both preaching (*kerygma*) and doctrine (*didache*).

A church may claim to be a part of the one, holy, apostolic, and universal church as a visible sociological organization. The authenticity of this claim, however, is validated "wherever the pure Word of God is preached and taught." Preaching and teaching of the pure Word of God are the signposts that a visible organization may authentically be called "the church of Jesus Christ." Conversely, where the pure Word of God is not preached, the true church does not exist.

THE SACRAMENTS OF THE CHURCH

Groups associated with the Protestant Reformation generally acknowledge two sacraments: baptism and Communion. These groups have accepted only two of the seven sacraments claimed by the Roman Catholic church. In his essay "Popery Calmly Considered," Wesley writes:

... wherever the Sacraments of Baptism and Holy Communion are celebrated in obedience to Christ's command ...

> The Church of Rome says, "A sacrament is a sensible thing, instituted by God himself, as a sign and a means of grace.
>
> "The sacraments are seven: Baptism, confirmation, the Lord's supper, penance, extreme unction, orders, and marriage.
>
> "The parts of a sacrament are, the matter, and the form, or words of consecration. So in baptism, the matter is water; the form, 'I baptize thee.' "[1]

By contrast, Wesley states his position:

> However, they teach that "all these seven confer grace *ex opere operato*, by the work itself, on all such as do not put an obstruction." Nay, it is not enough that we do not put an obstruction. In order to our receiving grace, there is also required previous instruction, true repentance, and a degree of faith; and even then the grace does not spring merely *ex opere operato*: It does not proceed from the mere elements, or the words spoken; but from the blessing of God, in consequence of his promise to such as are qualified for it.[2]

Wesley affirmed baptism and Holy Communion as the only sacraments. What God conveys through His grace is also,

145

as Wesley said, "a pledge of future glory."[3] The grace of Christ that the sacraments convey do not occur *ex opere operato:* there is no singular redemptive quality possessed by the wine (juice) or bread of communion or by the water of baptism.

Baptism sustains and nourishes believing souls. This is true for the worshiping congregation and the offering parents. Certainly the infant is more passive in baptism than the youth or adult acting to receive of the Lord's Supper. But baptism is a communion service; it is a means of receiving God's grace. In infant baptism, there is a specific emphasis on "the pledge of future glory." The congregation and the parents promise that they will so teach the child in the way of the Lord that, according to their best and faithful efforts, when the child achieves an age of personal maturity, he or she will confirm that the grace bestowed in infancy is fully appropriated. The sacrament of infant incorporation, or baptism, allows the child to partake of the community of the faithful. At such time as the child chooses to be incorporated into the community of faith, "confirmation" is the transitional act.[4]

In summary, infant baptism is a self-conscious theological act by parents and/or guardians and the local congregation under the inspiration of the Holy Spirit that incorporates a child into the kingdom of God. Youth therefore need not be rebaptized when confirmation training is complete. A person self-consciously accepts the invitation to become a full, participating member of a local congregation and a denomination in positive response to membership vows.

Infant dedication is a pledge, principally by the parents and/or guardians, to dedicate the child to God's purposes and to raise the infant in a manner that would support and facilitate that dedication. The infant is not, technically, a member of the church and is not baptized. When later a decision is made by the person to accept Christ and to participate fully in the church, baptism precedes the membership commitment. Confirmation training is the same in this case as for those who are baptized as infants. It is a training anticipatory to church membership vows. For the baptized infant, some would argue that confirmation training and the joining of a local congregation amount to reconfirmation. Likewise, some would contend that "once baptized, always baptized;" if one has been baptized as an infant then rebaptism at any age or stage of later spiritual maturity is inappropriate. Others claim that infant baptism does not involve the full faculties of the person that adult baptism would include. Therefore, the adult who has made a personal profession of faith should be afforded the rite of baptism as an affirmation of the fullness of a personal appropriation of faith and in anticipation of joining a local church, whether or not baptism in infancy can be ascertained.

In both baptism and Communion there is a similar dynamic interaction of memory, representation, and promise. The grace of Jesus Christ is being conveyed and communicated to the "communicant" both directly (as in Holy Communion where the person receives the elements) and indirectly (as in infant baptism or dedication where the person passively participates). An attitude of worship, humility, and hope—a full reverence—attends participation in the sacraments by all concerned.

THE SPIRITUALITY OF THE CHURCH

The Holy Spirit confers gifts on believers. There is a variety of gifts, among which are these: healing, the working of miracles, prophecy, utterance of wisdom, utterance of knowledge, faith, and speaking in tongues (1 Cor. 12:7–10).

... wherever the gifts of the Holy Spirit upbuild the body and bring spiritual growth ...

No gift constitutes a complete theological blessing. Those who seek to organize a group, a theology, or a subchurch around any particular gift clearly violate the spirit in which gifts are given. This interpretation is plainly taught and distilled from Scripture and the holistic nature of the church itself.

Clearly the Bible teaches that the fruit of the Spirit and the gifts of God are intended to unify and clarify. They not only bring certainty of doctrine but also facilitate spiritual and interpersonal growth among the various members of the body of Christ.

In brief, the gifts are given to increase the upbuilding of the body. They enhance one's experience of justification by faith and increase spiritual growth or sanctification, the perfecting of holiness.

THE FELLOWSHIP OF THE CHURCH

Evidence of the church's authenticity is in its ministry of specific acts of faithfulness in preaching, teaching, and partaking of the sacraments in loving obedience to the Lord Jesus Christ. In these acts the church conveys grace and discipleship.

. . . wherever the Spirit of God creates a loving, caring fellowship, and a faithfulness in witness and service to the world . . .

A loving and caring climate, created by the Holy Spirit, is a sign of the authenticity of the church. One may be thankful that the various denominations do not have a board whose responsibility is to program fellowship. Fellowship in Christ is created by the Holy Spirit and is an essential ingredient in church life. Christians need to love and care for one another. The warm milk of human kindness flows in the veins of the authentic church. The church is empowered and drawn toward the loving and caring spirit for its own membership. This is an authentic witness that testifies both to the church and to the watching world.

Clearly affirmed is the loving and caring fellowship, fully expressed in faithful witness and service outward toward the world and inward toward the believers.

The caring and loving fellowship expressed through witness and service extends beyond warm and compassionate interpersonal relationships. It includes sharing a cup of cold water in the name of Christ, clothing the naked, comforting the oppressed, and leading forth into new life and a new light a world that has not experienced the loving and caring relationships that abide in Christ and His church.

THE DISCIPLINE OF THE CHURCH

The church, in its faith, its internal service and care, and its witness and love in the world, needs discipline. The church has to retain or attain the capacity to say yes and to say no.

. . . and wherever discipline is administered with love under the guidance of the Word of God.

Discipline is simply a consistent way of relating to situations as they arise so that one has the capacity to say yes or no—and mean it.

In the contemporary church, discipline among many denominations and congregations is not very evident. Sporadic discipline frequently is coupled with overindulgence on petty matters. This approach reveals that a definite pattern is not practiced with consistency in church life. Discipline is consistent action; it is not punishment. Discipline is not punitive action; it is the making of disciples through training and development in godliness.

No may call forth feelings of anger, disappointment, hurt, and rejection—as though the believer is being punished and not disciplined. Spiritual temper tantrums indicate the failure of growth in holiness!

All discipline is to be qualified by love. Love and the teachings of God's Word provide the underlying consistency of the yes and no of the church. Discipline is properly administered with love when it is "under the guidance of the Word of God." This affirms the dual character of discipline. It flows from individual judgment and from the objective guidance of the Word of God.

Discipline is necessary and consistent with the gospel's call to love. Loving discipline is the guidance of the Word of God.

The church is empowered to say yes and to say no in

disciplined, consistent love. This is faithful to the scriptural understanding of the way God relates to the church.

THE TRIUMPH OF THE CHURCH

The Church is the bride of Christ and continues as one holy, apostolic, universal church. The authenticity of this church is found in the Word of God purely preached and taught; it is found in the sacraments of baptism and Communion; it is found in the loving and caring fellowship of the members of the church as expressed in faithful witness and service to the world; it is found in the discipline that permits the church to be drawn toward that occasion in which she will be joined with Jesus Christ her Lord in triumphant glory.

The Church, as the Bride of Christ, will ultimately be joined with her Lord in triumphant glory.

The triumphant union of Jesus Christ and the church will consummate the fullness of the church's life in sweet, eternal communion with Jesus Christ.

The church remembers her Lord; the church shows forth the authentic nature of her Lord; the church anticipates the fulfillment of the promise of the eternal union with her Lord.

DISCUSSION QUESTIONS

1. What does it mean to affirm the church as one, holy, apostolic, and universal? Is this too much for scriptural Christianity to affirm?

2. What is scriptural Christianity's perspective on a truly ecumenical church? Is it a possibility?

3. What is the authentic church?

4. Does the church, the body of Christ, amount to more or less than you thought? Why?

5. Do you belong to the church triumphant? Do you live as a sharer in the triumph of the church?

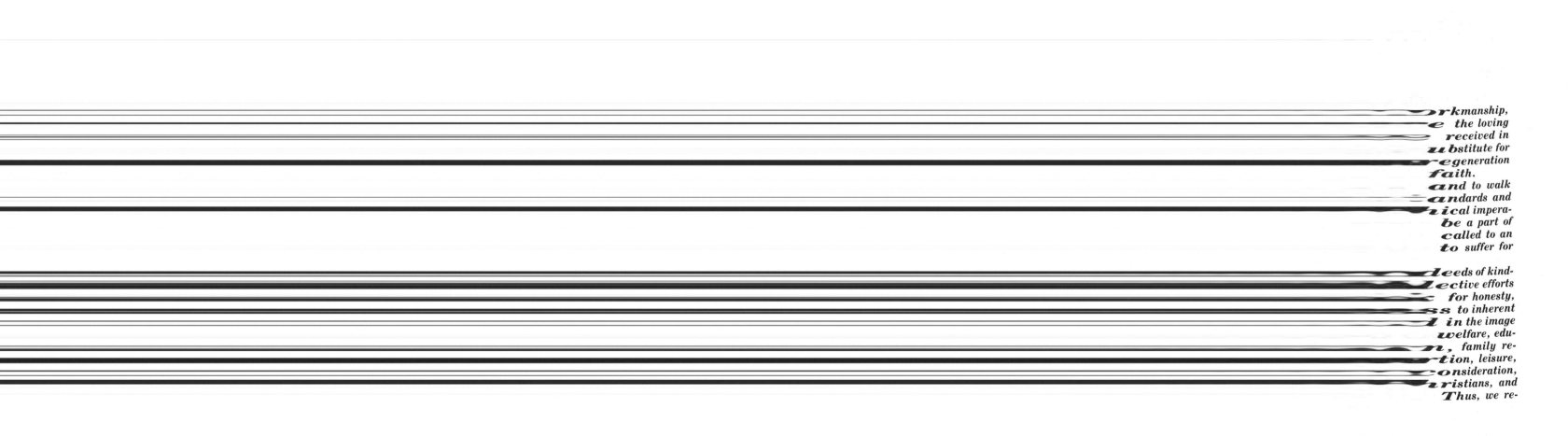

We are called to li —
components of Chri
the working out of th
holiness. *Thus, we*
dead."

The Christian life
without deep roots i
have been saved, th
selves, it is the gift
boast" (Eph. 2:8–9).
tion by faith alone.
on the redeeming g
ingenuity of human
even principally in
tends to make peopl
resources. This leads
will do all things wel
hand, the Bible is cl
faith alone, our faith
panied by good work

Faithfulness and H
in continual demand
long an artificial, un
ogy over the interloc
this chapter I will try
cate that faithfulness
faith and works. Fait
without faith are dea

CHRISTIANS A
The Christian joins
grace through faith (
tinues without except

Scriptural Christianity affir
we are God's workmanship,
in Christ Jesus for good wor

4. Does the church, the body of Christ, amount to more or less than you thought? Why?

5. Do you belong to the church triumphant? Do you live as a sharer in the triumph of the church?

ETHICS

Scriptural Christianity affirms that we are God's workmanship, created in Christ Jesus for good works. These works are the loving expressions of gratitude by the believer for the new life received in Christ. They do not earn one's salvation nor are they a substitute for God's work of redemption. Rather, they are the result of regeneration and are manifest in the believer as evidence of a living faith.

God has called us to do justice, to love kindness, and to walk humbly with Him. In the Scriptures are found the standards and principles that guide the believer in this walk. These ethical imperatives, willingly accepted by the believer, enable us to be a part of God's purposes in the world. Moreover, in this we are called to an obedience that does not stop short of our willingness to suffer for righteousness' sake, even unto death.

Our life in Christ includes an unstinting devotion to deeds of kindness and mercy and a wholehearted participation in collective efforts to alleviate need and suffering. The believer will work for honesty, justice and equity in human affairs; all of which witness to inherent rights and a basic dignity common to all persons created in the image of God. Such contemporary issues as racism, housing, welfare, education, Marxism, capitalism, hunger, crime, sexism, family relationships, aging, sexuality, drugs and alcohol, abortion, leisure, pornography, and related issues call for prayerful consideration, thoughtful analysis, and appropriate action from Christians, and must always be a matter of concern to the Church. Thus, we remember that faith without works is dead.

We are called to live by both faith and good works. These components of Christian experience are equally important in the working out of the believer's salvation, in the perfecting of holiness. *Thus, we remember that "faith without works is dead."*

The Christian life does not blossom from an ethical system without deep roots in an abiding faith. "For it is by grace you have been saved, through faith—and this is not from yourselves, it is the gift of God—not by works, so that no one can boast" (Eph. 2:8–9). We are saved in the initial phase of salvation by faith alone. We are always fundamentally dependent on the redeeming grace of God for salvation and not on the ingenuity of human, social engineering. Trusting alone or even principally in social contracts and human engineering tends to make people seek all power and authority in human resources. This leads to the utopian view that humans can and will do all things well and for the common good. On the other hand, the Bible is clear in this, that though we are saved by faith alone, our faith is never really alone; it is always accompanied by good works.

Faithfulness and holiness demonstrated in good works are in continual demand in the church and its ministry. For too long an artificial, unbiblical division has existed in our theology over the interlocking relation of faith and social action. In this chapter I will try to bring these halves together and indicate that faithfulness and holiness are the biblical balance of faith and works. Faith without works is dead—just as works without faith are dead.

CHRISTIANS ARE CREATED FOR GOOD WORKS

The Christian joins Paul in the belief that one is saved by grace through faith (Eph. 2:8). This mutual affirmation continues without exception; "For we are God's workmanship, created in Christ Jesus to do good works, which God prepared in advance for us to do"

Scriptural Christianity affirms that we are God's workmanship, created in Christ Jesus for good works.

(v. 10). Christians are a new creation in Christ (2 Cor. 5:17). Intrinsic to this new creation is an inspired, Christ-directed response: doing good works. Our vocation as believers is to serve and witness in the good works that God has set before us.

The Scripture teaches that good works are not optional for the believer. Neither do they come automatically to new creatures in Christ. Good works come through purposeful discipline to witness in word and deed. However, there is indeed an obligatory character about good works in Christ.[1] All Christians are called to do good works as an expression and measure of the good work God through Jesus Christ is doing in them.

GOOD WORKS EXPRESS GRATITUDE

The motivation for good works flows fully from the believer's holy gratitude. They spring forth from a loving, caring, compassionate, faithful concern for others, directed and mellowed by the holiness of God's grace. Good works are a response to, and an expression of, the new creation; they are not plea bargaining for salvation. A concise review of the theological sequence of salvation and good works can be outlined: (1) sin, (2) justification, and (3) sanctification and good works. Good works are the perfecting of holiness; not the beginning.

These works are the loving expressions of gratitude by the believer for the new life received in Christ. They do not earn one's salvation nor are they a substitute for God's work of redemption.

GOOD WORKS RESULT FROM FAITH

The Christian's vocation to good works is not to be misconstrued or misinterpreted as an endorsement of humanization as a substitute for Christianization. The primary call is to redemption (Christianization) and then to emancipation (humanization). But the two

Rather, they are the result of regeneration and are manifest in the believer as evidence of a living faith.

155

are not to be confused; nor are they interchangeable. To help preserve the necessary distinctions, the word *rather* was selected in order to guard against false or misleading interpretations.

For the Christian, living is becoming Christlike; the believer's life undergoes the discipline of increasing conformity to the image of Christ. One is to live in imitation of Christ. Good works, therefore, are not solely the effort to establish a good civil order or to hasten the coming of the secular good life. For the Christian, good works evidence and exemplify the church and the believer becoming like Christ. Good works are the working out the final perfection, fullness, and completion of salvation; they are integral to new life in Christ Jesus. But they do not precede new life in Christ. Good works do not exist independently of new life in Christ. They flow out of the unity that the believer has with Christ. "I have been crucified with Christ and I no longer live, but Christ lives in me" (Gal. 2:20).

GOD HAS CALLED US TO DO GOOD WORKS

The Old Testament lays the foundation for New Testament good works (Mic. 6:8). The evidence of a living faith is found in the response of doing justice, loving kindness, and acting with humility. Donald Bloesch correctly reminds us of the primacy of the church's mandate: "In addition to pronouncing woe upon injustice wherever it may be found, the truly prophetic church will reveal the way of God more perfectly by suggesting alternatives to specific sinful practices."[2]

God has called us to do justice, to love kindness, and to walk humbly with Him.

The Christian is not called to maintain a positive attitude about or to meditate on justice, kindness, and humility. The Scriptures teach what believers and the community of the faithful are to do: they are to love and they are to walk. These are activities of faithfulness. These are behavioral evidences of the lived faith, of being ambassadors of Christ. Doing justice, loving kindness, and walking humbly characterize the chosen people of God; those born of God's covenant are to hold out hope for a better life by what they believe and do. The church is to live out being children of God. Genuine faith will show itself in action.

SCRIPTURE CALLS FOR GOOD WORKS

Justice, kindness, and humility are the social imperatives of redeemed behavior. They are the good works of the righteous. For the Christian, social action and social service do not begin, nor find their fulfillment, in themselves. Good works are located in and flow from God. God in Christ obligates the church to act in specific and concrete acts of social service. The standards and principles that guide good works are precisely justice, kindness, and humility. These standards and principles are clearly revealed in, or are plainly established as truth by, the Scriptures.

In the Scriptures are found the standards and principles that guide the believer in this walk.

BELIEVERS BEAR GOD'S BURDEN IN GOOD WORKS

These ethical imperatives, willingly accepted by the believer, enable us to be a part of God's purposes in the world.

Good works are indeed imperatives for the believer and the community of believers. They are obligations. Good works are a vocation. Faith without works is dead.

With a loving heart one willingly accepts the discipline of participating in God's purposes in the world. The community of believers bears the burdens of God's will and the burdens of the world. There is renewing power in God's purpose. God empowers believers to participate in His loving and caring relationship within creation, to call into judgment, to redeem, and to emancipate.

157

GOOD WORKS ARE FOR REAL

Life in Christ is no pipe dream; it is for real. The word *moreover* emphasizes the utmost seriousness of God's call to do justice, to love kindness, and to walk humbly. Justice, kindness, and humility in action are lively evidences of a living faith.

Moreover, in this we are called to an obedience that does not stop short of our willingness to suffer for righteousness' sake, even unto death.

The Scriptures either plainly reveal or clearly teach those standards and principles that should guide our behavior. God wants believers to share in the joy of participating in His continuing efforts to redeem the world and to perfect holiness in creation through emancipation from spiritual and social evil. The vitality of a living faith and the magnitude of good works show themselves in an energetic participation in justice, kindness, and humility. Christians are to be obedient and faithful to the end.

The root meaning of *obey* is "to hear." Therefore obedience means that one truly hears God's call. In affirming the Christian vocation and discipleship of good works in Christ, one obeys the call to discipleship to whatever end God calls. The capacity to hear, and therefore to obey, extends through the whole range of participation in God's purposes in the world. It includes suffering for the sake of the kingdom, if need be; and suffering may extend to death.

Remember the word *moreover*. It suggests that believers ought not to be surprised that God's gift of suffering may include death. Christians are not called to shallow platitudes or symbolic, token gestures of good intention. The call is to give full evidence of life in Christ, even in the deep waters of life and in the valley of the shadow of death. Christians are called to be ready to suffer even to the extent of giving their lives. The call is not to radical rhetoric but to radical obedience.

GOOD WORKS ARE OUR IDENTITY

The call to justice, kindness, and humility follows from ethical imperatives willingly accepted in faithfulness and holiness. In the call to a radical obedience, good works flow directly into deeds (specific activities) of kindness, of mercy, and of wholehearted participation.

Our life in Christ includes an unstinting devotion to deeds of kindness and mercy and a wholehearted participation in collective efforts to alleviate need and suffering.

God calls Christians to unreserved obedience and faithful responsiveness. He calls by ethical imperatives to good works. Wholehearted participation in deeds of kindness and mercy is to be complete and whole; it is our redemption!

A wholehearted redemption is evidenced in wholehearted deeds. Wholehearted good works are evidence of being perfected in holiness.

The deeds believers are called to participate in without reservation and with complete devotion may be individual activities of kindness and mercy. But clearly we affirm that pre-eminent participation for the community of believers occurs in *collective efforts:* the call to alleviate need and suffering.

The evangelical has a corporate, social call in Christ. One's identity in Christ is a social relation. The body of Christ is an organism and society in the world. The world itself, of course, is an organism and a society internally related to God, as is the church.

As individuals, Christians are social beings. Therefore, individual good works "hit their stride" in active participation in collective efforts. We are social and corporate beings. Collective activities are the essence of the Christian life; they are how good works are supremely expressed.

GOOD WORKS ARE DIRECTED TOWARD PEOPLE

The ethical imperative is willingly and graciously received by the believer. The imperative tells what the Christian *will* do. The believer, without hesitancy, works "for honesty, justice,

159

The believer will work for honesty, justice and equity in human affairs . . . and equity in human affairs." The Christian is called to hear and to obey. God requires that believers devote significant periods of time to research, reflection, discussion, and education about the dynamic realities involved in human affairs. This is stated to affirm that the believer, in fact, works and participates in good works.

There is a time for talking and there is a time for doing. The evangelical acts because the creative transformation in Jesus Christ creates in us the will to work for honesty, justice, and equity in human affairs. Apart from good works, there is no salvation. It is that simple. Faith without works is dead.

GOOD WORKS ENHANCE PERSONAL DIGNITY

Believers are called to wholehearted participation in particular efforts to alleviate need and suffering. We are called to "deeds of kindness and mercy." The motivation is always theological because we affirm that "all persons [are] created in the image of God."

. . . all of which witness to inherent rights and a basic dignity common to all persons created in the image of God.

God calls the church to minister to all humanity, and all humanity is created in God's image. We want to witness faithfully to the inherent rights and basic dignities common to all humanity.

The Christian lives with the ethical imperative to participate with God to bring about righteousness, justice, kindness, and humility.

GOOD WORKS ARE FOR SERVICE AND REFORM

Such contemporary issues as racism, housing, welfare, education, Marxism, capitalism, hunger, crime, sexism, family relationships, aging, sexuality, drugs and alcohol, abortion, leisure, pornography, and related issues . . .

Christians are called to radical obedience and to join in battle with specific concrete realities that confront "God's workmanship, created in Christ Jesus to do good works" (Eph. 2:10).

The above list suggests some of the major contemporary issues for the community of believers, the church of Jesus Christ. These contemporary issues will not abide forever, at least in their present forms. Some of them will ease in time, whereas some of them may intensify in the future. The concern in this study is to focus on those issues that are recognized as serious problems. These are not the only issues properly before Christ's church, but they are representative. And they are current problems.

These issues confront the church in three major areas: (1) society, (2) family, and (3) persons. Specific program responses will not be detailed because this is a theological affirmation not a program-agency agenda. Some issues are clearly defined as evil, whereas other issues require thorough investigation to determine the actual causes and effects. Without such investigation precipitous action, immature judgment, and vain rhetoric result. Such action would distract from God's ethical imperatives and would destroy wholehearted participation and faithful witness to the rights and dignity common to all persons.

Christians are called to a measured and mature response. This is a painful and agonizing call to mature and sober reflection. God's call is not to precipitous action nor to vain and heated arguments that fall short of credibility and charity. It is a call to a radical obedience to the radical gospel of God's gracious salvation to them that believe.

These contemporary issues permeate our social and institutional systems. They are of urgent concern to the believer because "the corruption of sin" extends into "societal systems, and all creation."[3] These issues challenge obedience to Christ because the Christian is God's workmanship and called to good works in the social, corporate, and systematic ideological dimensions of life. However, these issues cannot be understood nor can they be addressed with appropriate reflection and discerning judgment apart from full recognition of their societal, collective, and corporate dimensions.

In the smaller, collective, and corporate societies and systems identified as family relationships, there are many deep problems. As a result of "the Fall of Adam the corruption of sin has pervaded every person and extended into social relationships."[4] The primary social relationships in American culture are family relationships. God's concern for the "little societies" calls believers and the church to good works, wholehearted participation, and a willing obedience to God's redemptive purposes among family relationships. Family problems are social as well as personal. Regardless of its fragmented nature, each family is, in its relationships, a mini-social system. The family cannot be understood or properly addressed nor can redemptive action be initiated in isolation from helping the family as a social unit. The principal social/personal concerns involved include at least family relationships, aging, and sexuality.

Societal systems and social relationships are also permeated by problems of artificial stimulants, narcissism, forceful ending of life, greed, and lust. Adam's fall has in fact extended corruption to personal relationships, including the motivation for drugs and alcohol, abortion, leisure, and pornography. Individuals, like families and the church, are organisms. They are bound in societal systems, social relationships, and personal interactions. Problems that permeate and haunt personal relations cannot be addressed, resolved, or understood apart from understanding societal systems and social relations. The faithful believer must make a wholehearted effort to resolve these problems.

The sixteen issues delienated thus far do not exhaust by any means the important ethical concerns that confront the church. Many other related issues have their unique manifestations and particularities. No single ethical issue can be isolated and treated as if it were unrelated to any other issue. The problems that confront the human family are bound ultimately to a struggle that languishes under the Adamic curse.

GOOD WORKS REQUIRE PRAYER, THOUGHT, AND CONCERN

The initial response to social issues calls for "prayerful consideration." The obedient re-
lationship to God compels one
to do justice, love kindness,
and walk humbly with God.
This is an outgrowth of full participation in God's purposes in the world.

. . . call for prayerful consideration, thoughtful analysis, and appropriate action from Christians, and must always be a matter of concern to the Church.

Initially one enters that relationship in prayerful consideration. The Christian wants to submit the issues to God and to
struggle over them in intelligent, attentive praying. Prayers
are not to be empty and vain. These problems are not to be
dismissed with an easy, polite gesture, as though they belong
solely to God. Ours is to be a considered, measured, disciplined struggle in prayer.

Turning prayerfully to God about these matters calls for a
patient waiting on God for a response. This includes asking
God how a willingness to help may be expressed in loving
deeds of kindness and mercy. Prayerful consideration is
a reverent openness toward God, asking divine guidance
for understanding and insight about specific, concrete,
and deliberate "collective efforts to alleviate need and
suffering."[5]

In addition to prayerful consideration that brings about a
spiritual wrestling with these problems, the evangelical believes that God calls for an honest, full, forthright, intellectual
struggle to "think through" human concerns and problems.
The believer is called on to achieve an intellectually responsible understanding of, and plan of action for, good works.
Prayerful consideration is essential, and thoughtful analysis is
necessary.

The process is to carry the concerns to God in prayer that
believers may be more fully perfected in holiness and brought
into harmony with the Godhead as they continue in good
works in Jesus Christ. Initially these problems are perceived

as spiritual concerns, as suggested by Scripture. Next, the believer pursues the problem toward an intellectual level of understanding. Putting the spiritual and intellectual insights together requires thoughtful and deliberate plans for action. And action it must be. This is the good-works paradigm.

Appropriate action inevitably and inseparably follows from adequate prayerful considerations and intellectual analyses. Faith without works is dead; works without faith are dead also.

Prayerful consideration without action is vain piety. Intellectual analysis without action is intellectualism. As new creations in Christ, Christians are called to marshal all the spiritual, intellectual, and psychological power available and focus it on appropriate action. Marshaling and mobilizing spiritual considerations and intellectual analyses leads to theologically appropriate action!

The inescapable claim for good works is always with Christ's church. The phrase "must always be" displays the strongest wording possible. All other statements thus far are descriptive or declarative. In no other place in the Affirmation does one find words like *should, ought,* or *must.* All the other expressions of affirmation of the essentials of Wesleyan theology are statements, declarations, or clarifications.

The strongest language, the most forthright and compelling exhortation to ethical imperatives, is reserved for good works. This language helps to affirm that the issues listed above and their related concerns are inescapably and always a matter of responsible action by the church. Where these issues are not experienced as such imperatives, they must become so. Spiritual and social sensitivity is a matter of utmost urgency for Christians because they are created in Christ for good works.

The call to good works carries with it the blessings and the risks that attend any call to full participation in God's activity of salvation, the fellowship of the sacraments, or the good works of perfecting holiness.

There is a threefold call and imperative for the perfecting of holiness. This call "must always be a matter of concern to the Church." God calls the Church (1) to conform increasingly to the image of Christ, (2) to share abundantly and faithfully in the kingdom that is the work and life of the Holy Spirit, and (3) to become more intimately involved in the whole family of God, witnessing to the inherent rights and basic dignities of all persons.

The concerns to which we are called are not individual problems solely nor family concerns solely. Neither are they Sunday-school-class concerns or congregational concerns exclusively. Rather, they are concerns for the church, the body of Christ, in all their social and personal complexity.

The call to good works is heard obediently by individual Christians, who are to act wholeheartedly in collective and corporate efforts in the life of the church universal. The church is a living organism (a living body) and extends to societal systems (juridical, educational, legislative, economic, moral), family relationships, personal interactions—in short, to all creation. Without this call to boldness in corporate witness, the force and energy of individual prayers, thoughtful analyses, and efforts to act will, indeed, fall short!

GOOD WORKS VALIDATE FAITH

The conclusion is a preamble: justification and sanctification are inseparable. Good works and a new creation in Christ are inseparable. Obedience to God's call is inseparable from suffering for righteousness' sake.

Thus, we remember that faith without works is dead.

Appropriate action is inseparable from prayerful consideration and thoughtful analysis. Prayerful consideration is inseparable from thoughtful analysis and appropriate action. Thoughtful analysis is inseparable from prayerful consideration and appropriate action.

All of these are expressions of the fact that good works

165

must be an integral part of the Christian life; apart from good works salvation itself can be seriously questioned.[6]

Again, let it be said and heard: "Faith without deeds is dead" (James 2:26).

DISCUSSION QUESTIONS

1. Why are we taught that faith without works is dead and that there is no salvation apart from good works?

2. Do you believe that evangelicals are lax in their witness in the area of good works? Why or why not?

3. What do you think of the threefold emphasis on (1) social, (2) family, and (3) personal areas of ethical concerns?

4. Are you willing to accept an obedience that does not stop short of our willingness to suffer for righteousness' sake, even to the extent of dying?

5. What are ethical imperatives? How do they operate for the scriptural Christian?

Notes

PREAMBLE

[1]See the *Perkins Journal*, 28, no. 1 (Fall 1974). The entire volume is given over to a discussion of the 1972 revision of *The Discipline*. Included are articles by Frederic Herzog, "United Methodism in Agony?"; Leroy T. Howe, "United Methodism in Search of Theology"; and Schubert M. Ogden, "Doctrinal Standards in the United Methodist Church." See also Robert L. Cushman, "Church Doctrinal Standards Today," *Religion in Life* (Fall 1975), pp. 401–11; P. Dale Neufer, "Creedal Freedom in American Methodism," *Religion in Life* (Spring 1974), pp. 42–51; Robert E. Coleman, "The New Doctrinal Directives of Methodism" (an unpublished paper); Robert Kuhn, "Theological Pluralism: Today's Liberal Charade," *Christianity Today* (29 August 1975), p. 51; "Making Pluralism Real," editorial, *Good News* (April–June 1972), pp. 61–62; Larry Eisenberg, "What Are the 'Limits' of Pluralism? Here I Stand, But a Bit Confused," *The United Methodist Reporter* (26 December 1975), p. 2; "Letters to the Editor," *The United Methodist Reporter* (13 September 1974), p. 2.

[2]Richard F. Lovelace, "Unitive Evangelicalism" (an unpublished paper, Gordon-Conwell Seminary), p. 17. See also, Donald Dayton, *Discovering an Evangelical Heritage* (San Francisco: Harper and Row, 1976); Peter L. Berger and Richard John Neuhaus, eds., "The Hartford Appeal" (of 1975), *Against the World for the Word* (New York: Seabury, 1976).

[3]Carl F. H. Henry, *God, Revelation, and Authority* (Waco: Word, 1976); Rene Padilla, ed., *The New Face of Evangelicalism* (Downers Grove, Ill.: InterVarsity, 1977); Jack Rogers, *Biblical Authority* (Waco: Word, 1976); Richard Mouw, *Politics and the Biblical Drama* (Grand Rapids: Eerdmans, 1976); Bernard Ramm, *The Evangelical Heritage* (Waco: Word, 1973); and Donald Bloesch, *Essentials of Evangelical Theology*, vols. 1 and 2 (New York: Harper and Row, 1978).

2

THE HOLY TRINITY

[1]John Wesley, "On the Trinity," in *The Works of John Wesley*, 14 vols. (1872; reprint ed, Grand Rapids: Zondervan, 1958–59), 6:199.

[2]Ibid. p. 205.

[3]Ibid. p. 201.

[4]Wesley, "Catholic Spirit," *Works*, 5:494.

[5]Ibid., p. 497.

[6]John Calvin, *Institutes of the Christian Religion*, trans. Ford Lewis Battles, vol. XX of the *Library of Christian Classics*, ed. J. T. McNeill (Philadelphia: Westminster, 1960), I.13.1, pp. 120–21.

[7]Ibid., p. 122.

[8]Wesley, "On the Trinity," *Works*, 6:203.

[9]John B. Cobb, Jr., *Christ in a Pluralistic Age* (Philadelphia: Westminster, 1975), p. 261.

[10]Cobb says, "However, neuterization is a high price to pay for neutrality, and in any case, it will not suffice. The Logos is indissolubly bound up with Christ, and because Jesus was Christ, Christ must be referred to as 'He'" (ibid., p. 263).

[11]Calvin, *Institutes*, I.13.3, p. 123.

[12]Henry Bettenson, ed., *Documents of the Christian Church*, 2nd ed. (London: Oxford University Press, 1963), p. 46.

[13]Calvin, *Institutes*, I.13.2, p. 123.

[14]Wesley, "On the Trinity," *Works*, 6:204.

3

GOD THE FATHER

[1]John Wesley, "The Unity of Divine Being," in *The Works of John Wesley*, 14 vols. (1872; reprint ed., Grand Rapids: Zondervan, 1958–59), 7:265–73.

[2]Ibid., p. 265.

[3]Ibid., pp. 265–66.

[4]Wesley, "On Divine Providence," *Works*, 6:315.

[5]Ibid., p. 316.

[6]Ibid., p. 318.

[7]John Calvin, *Institutes of the Christian Religion*, trans. Ford Lewis

Battles, vol. XX of the *Library of Christian Classics*, ed. J. T. McNeill (Philadelphia: Westminster, 1960), I.13.2, p. 122.

[8]Wesley, "Spiritual Worship," *Works*, pp. 424–27.

[9]Calvin, *Institutes*, I.10.2, pp. 97–98.

[10]Wesley, "God's Love to Fallen Man," *Works*, 6:234.

[11]Wesley, "Unity of Divine Being," *Works*, p. 269.

[12]Ibid.

4

GOD THE SON

[1]John Calvin, *Institutes of the Christian Religion*, trans. Ford Lewis Battles, vol. XX of the *Library of Christian Classics*, ed. J. T. McNeill (Philadelphia: Westminster, 1960), II.14.1, p. 482.

[2]Ibid., II.13.4, p. 481.

[3]*Westminster Dictionary of the Bible* (Philadelphia: Westminster, 1944), p. 29.

[4]Calvin, *Institutes*, II.15.2, p. 496.

[5]Ibid., II.15.6., p. 502.

5

GOD THE HOLY SPIRIT

[1]John Wesley, "On the Holy Spirit," in *The Works of John Wesley*, 14 vols. (1872; reprint ed., Grand Rapids: Zondervan, 1958–59), 7:509.

[2]John Calvin, *Institutes of the Christian Religion*, trans. Ford Lewis Battles, vol. XX in the *Library of Christian Classics*, ed. J. T. McNeill (Philadelphia: Westminster, 1960), III.3.1, p. 592.

[3]Wesley, "Journal" (Oct. 14, 1735 to Nov. 29, 1745; entry for May 24, 1738), *Works*, 1:103.

[4]Wesley, "Scriptural Christianity," *Works*, 5:38.

[5]Wesley, "On the Holy Spirit," *Works*, 7:517.

6

HUMANITY

[1]John Wesley, "Original Sin," in *The Works of John Wesley*, 14 vols. (1872; reprint ed., Grand Rapids: Zondervan, 1958–59), 6:56–57.
[2]Ibid., p. 60.
[3]Ibid.
[4]Ibid., 6:57–59; 7:61.

7

THE HOLY SCRIPTURES

[1]*The Articles of Religion of The Methodist Church* (1784); *The Book of Discipline of The United Methodist Church* (Nashville: United Methodist Publishing House, 1976), p. 56.
[2]John Calvin, *Institutes of the Christian Religion*, trans. Ford Lewis Battles, vol. XX of the *Library of Christian Classics*, ed. John T. McNeill (Philadelphia: Westminster, 1960), I.7.1, p. 74.
[3]Ibid., III.2.33, pp. 580–81.
[4]Ibid., I.6.1, p. 70.
[5]Ibid., I.6.2, p. 71.
[6]Ibid., I.7.4, p. 78.
[7]Ibid., p. 79.
[8]Ibid., III.2.6, p. 549.
[9]Ibid., I.6.2, p. 72.
[10]Harold Lindsell, *The Battle for the Bible* (Grand Rapids: Zondervan, 1976), see especially chapter 1, "Inerrancy an Evangelical Problem"; chapter 8, "Deviations That Follow When Inerrancy Is Denied." For a critique of the appeal to "inerrancy alone," see Stephen T. Davis, *The Debate About the Bible: Inerrancy Versus Infallibility* (Philadelphia: Westminster, 1977), especially chapter 5, "The Case Against Inerrancy."
[11]Thomas C. Oden, *Agenda for Theology* (N. Y.: Harper and Row, 1978), p. 29.
[12]Ibid., chapter 3.
[13]Ibid., p. 58.
[14]Stephen T. Davis, *The Debate About the Bible* (Philadelphia: Westminster, 1977), pp. 38–39.
[15]Donald G. Bloesch, *Essentials of Evangelical Theology*, Vol. I (N. Y.: Harper and Row, 1978), p. 66.

16 Ibid., p. 67.

17 See Donald W. Dayton, " 'The Battle for the Bible': Renewing the Inerrancy Debate," *The Christian Century* (10 November 1976), pp. 976–80; John H. Gerstner, "Warfield's Case for Biblical Inerrancy," in *God's Inerrant Word: An International Symposium on the Trustworthiness of Scripture*, ed. John Warwick Montgomery (Minneapolis: Bethany Fellowship, 1974), pp. 115–42. Also, Donald Dayton "Evangelical Contradictions," review of *The Evangelicals: What They Believe, Who They Are, Where They Are Going*, ed. D. F. Wells and J. D. Woodbridge (Nashville: Abingdon, 1975) in *Sojourners* (April 1976) pp. 24–26, and "Wells/Woodbridge and Don Dayton," *Sojourners* (September 1976), pp. 29, 31–32, 38.

18 Donald W. Dayton, *Discovering an Evangelical Heritage* (San Francisco: Harper and Row, 1976), p. 121. See the entire chapter, "Whatever Happened to Evangelicalism?" pp. 121–35 and "Epilogue: Reflections on Some Unresolved Issues," pp. 137–41. Evangelical Presbyterian pastor Stephen T. Davis, professor of philosophy and religion at Claremont Men's College, has written an illuminating volume, *The Debate About the Bible* (see note 10), from a philosophical and theological perspective. In it he endeavors to demonstrate the logical and experiential absurdity of hyper-Calvinistic scholasticism as a hermeneutic for contemporary American evangelicals.

19 See Alfred North Whitehead, *Process and Reality* (N. Y.: Macmillan, 1929), part III, chapter 1, "Feelings," pp. 334–60.

20 See Charles Hartshorne, *The Divine Relativity* (New Haven: Yale University Press, 1948). He explores rather fully the relationship of God's perfection and perfectibility.

21 Jack B. Rogers and Donald K. McKim, *The Authority and Interpretation of the Bible* (N. Y., Harper & Row, 1979), p. 383.

22 Ibid., p. 382.

23 John A. T. Robinson, *Re-Dating the New Testament* (Philadelphia: Westminster, 1976) p. 352. Here the argument, recently advanced, places the entire New Testament in the period of 40–70 A.D.

24 Robinson states, "There is no necessary correlation between the wealth of knowledge the documents can be made to yield about their setting in the life of the church and the *duration* of the period for which these processes give evidence. In logic this is obvious. Yet the 'tunnel period' between the events of the life, death, and resurrection of Jesus and the movement when, as it were, the train emerges, laden with ecclesiastical baggage, in our canonical documents has been viewed as so extended that almost anything could have happened on the way. . . . But obviously there is less likelihood of distortion the shorter the interval. . . . It is worth reminding New Testament theologians of the friendly chiding they have received, for instance, from the classical historian Sherwin-White for not

recognizing, by any contemporary standards, what excellent sources they have" (ibid., p. 355).

[25]Bernard Ramm, *Protestant Biblical Interpretation* (Boston: Wilde, 1950), p. 64–77.

[26]Cf. John W. Montgomery, "Lessons from Luther on the Inerrancy of Holy Writ," in *God's Inerrant Word*, ed. J. W. Montgomery (Minneapolis: Bethany Fellowship, 1973), p. 81.

8

SALVATION

[1]John Wesley, "Original Sin," in *The Works of John Wesley*, 14 vols. (1872; reprint ed., Grand Rapids: Zondervan, 1958–59), 6:59.

[2]Many associated with local churches and church leadership are creatively and therapeutically involved in group and interpersonal relationships where "processing" anger is considered a beneficial goal. The claim made is that people hold in anger and will not identify their own angry feelings. This denial distracts from and destroys the capacity for becoming "whole persons."

We need to learn to work productively with wrath and anger in strictly human relations. Why should we go about denying wrath and anger as appropriate relational feelings and behaviors for God? The issue facing those who oppose a theology that affirms the reality and dynamics of anger in God is simple. Why invest all the time, energy, and money in rediscovering, claiming, and working productively with human anger and at the same time withhold time, energy, and money from exploring the existence of and interpersonal promise for anger in the Godhead and in one's saving faith?

It is unwise to ignore the Scriptures and human experience. Instead of denying the reality of God's wrath and anger, follow the lead of Jesus the Son who faced the realities of wrath and anger on the cross. In Him all are invited to move from denial to salvation.

[3]Wesley, "The General Spread of the Gospel," *Works*, 6:281.

[4]Wesley discusses these points in his sermon "Of Hell," *Works*, 6:381, 383, 384, 390.

9

THE CHURCH

[1]John Wesley, "Popery Calmly Considered," in *The Works of John Wesley*, 14 vols. (1872; reprint ed., Grand Rapids: Zondervan, 1958–59), 10:149.

[2]Ibid.

[3]*The Eucharistic Manuals of John and Charles Wesley*, ed. with Introduction by W. E. Dutton (London: Bull, Simmons, 1871), p. 59.

[4]Mack B. Stokes, *Major United Methodist Beliefs*, rev. ed. (Nashville: Abingdon, 1971), p. 119.

10

ETHICS

[1]James M. Gustafson, *Can Ethics Be Christian?* (Chicago: University of Chicago Press, 1975).

[2]Donald G. Bloesch, *Essentials of Evangelical Theology* (New York: Harper and Row, 1979), 2:169.

[3]"The Junaluska Affirmation," section on "Humanity."

[4]Ibid.

[5]Ibid., section on "Ethics."

[6]Robert E. Cushman, "Fifty Years of Theology and Theological Education at Duke: Retrospect and Prospect" *The Duke Divinity School Review* (Winter 1977), pp. 21–22, says of John Wesley: "He was, of course, clear about man the sinner. But, in the hotly controverted *Conference Minutes* of 1770, Wesley scandalized the Calvinists of his day by declaring that 'works meet for repentance' are the inescapable obligation and outcome of justification and, further, if absent, absent too is the 'condition' of salvation. This let loose probably the most formidable doctrinal debate of the 18th century, between John Fletcher, against antinomianism, and Augustus Toplady and others. In plain words, Wesley had flown in the face of reformed theology simply to stand firm with the words of our Lord, 'By their fruits ye shall know them.' With Wesley, 'Christian perfection' was not optional. It was part of the doctrine with which the Methodists began and heedlessness to which might incur the sectarian deadness he feared most."

Indexes

Index of Persons

Albright, Jacob, 24
Augustine, Saint, 123

Barth, Karl, 60
Bettenson, Henry, 40–41
Bloesch, Donald, 156
Bultmann, Rudolf, 60

Calvin, John, 24, 34–35, 39, 41–42, 49, 56–57,
    59–60, 71, 97–102, 112, 121, 128, 131
Cobb, John B., Jr., 168
Cushman, Robert E., 173

Davis, Stephen T., 171

Edwards, Jonathan, 111

Kempis, Thomas `a, 89
Knox, John, 24

Lindsay, Thomas, 118
Luther, Martin, 24, 112, 120–21, 131

Magdalene, Mary, 131
McKim, Donald K., 118
McNeill, J.T., 34, 39, 56, 98, 101

Oden, Thomas, 110, 112
Otterbein, Philip, 24

Paul, apostle, 81, 89, 133, 141, 154
Peter, apostle, 71, 88, 132, 143

Robinson, James A. T., 171–72
Rogers, Jack B., 118

Stone, Samuel J., 141

Index of Subjects

Anger, 125, 128–31, 136, 149. *See also* Wrath.
Anointing, 58–59, 69–70
Apostles' Creed, 13, 24
Articles of Religion (Wesley), 14, 96
Atonement, 60–62, 64, 133

Baptism, 142, 146–47
Body of Christ. *See* Church.

Church, 16, 31, 37, 40–41, 46, 63, 71, 74, 75, 89,
   110, 134, 139–51, 165
Confession of Faith, 14
Conviction, 85–86, 112
Covenant, 14, 37, 49–52, 58, 69, 133, 157
Creeds, 25, 31. *See also* Apostles' Creed; Nicene
   Creed.

Deliverance, 51, 127. *See also* Redemption.
Didache, 144

Ethics, 153–66
Evangelical(s), 13, 22ff., 43, 46, 74. 94, 107–8,
   111–13, 159.
Evangelical United Brethren, 14, 26
Evil, 51, 63, 82–83, 129
Experience, 112, 113–14, 116, 117, 131, 133
Explanatory Notes upon the New Testament
   (Wesley), 13

Forgiveness, 62, 71–73, 87, 134

God the Father, 44, 45–52, 56, 95, 105, 117
God the Holy Spirit, 15, 64, 67–78, 85, 95, 105–6,
   148, 165
God the Son, 15, 55–65, 95
Good works, 154–66

Index of Scripture References